BATSFORD'S
Edinburgh
THEN AND NOW

BATSFORD'S
Edinburgh
THEN AND NOW

Jennifer Veitch

BATSFORD

First published in the United Kingdom in 2009 by
Batsford
10 Southcombe Street
London
W14 0RA

An imprint of Anova Books Company Ltd

ISBN 978-1-906388-37-9

A CIP catalogue record for this book is available from the British Library.

16 15 14 13 12 11 10 09
10 9 8 7 6 5 4 3 2 1

Reproduction by Rival Colour Limited, U.K.
Printed and bound by 1010 Printing International Limited, China

This book can be ordered direct from the publisher at the website: www.anovabooks.com

AUTHOR'S ACKNOWLEDGEMENTS
I am indebted to the earlier research carried out by C.S. Minto for his book, *Victorian and Edwardian Edinburgh from Old Photographs*, published in 1973. Thanks must go to the Balmoral Hotel and the Rutland Hotel for their help in securing the best vantage points of the city centre.

PHOTO CREDITS
The publisher wishes to thank SCRAN (Scottish Cultural Resources Access Network) for kindly providing 'then' photographs for the following pages: 6 (Patrick Geddes Centre for Planning Studies, University of Edinburgh), 18 (The Scotsman Publications Ltd), 22 (Marius Alexander), 26 (The Scotsman Publications Ltd), 30 (The Scotsman Publications Ltd), 46 (The Scotsman Publications Ltd), 48 (Royal Commission on the Ancient and Historical Monuments of Scotland), 50 (Edinburgh City Libraries), 52 (Paul Carwardine), 106 (The Scotsman Publications Ltd), 108 (The Scotsman Publications Ltd), 110, 114 (The Scotsman Publications Ltd), 118 inset (National Museums Scotland), 120 (The Scotsman Publications Ltd), 122 (The Scotsman Publications Ltd), 124 (The Scotsman Publications Ltd), 126 (The Scotsman Publications Ltd), 136 (Royal Commission on the Ancient and Historical Monuments of Scotland), 140 main (Napier University), 140 inset (The Owen Estate), 142 (St Andrews University Library).

All other 'then' photographs are courtesy of Anova Image Library.

Thanks to David Watts for taking all the 'now' photographs in this book, with the exception of the following pages: 19, 25 inset, 27, 31, 45, 49, 121, 123, 139, which were taken by Jennifer Veitch.

Pages 1 and 3 show: Grassmarket and Edinburgh Castle, then (photo: Anova Image Library) and now (photo: David Watts).

Front and back covers show: Princes Street from Scott Monument, then (photo: Anova Image Library) and now (photo: David Watts).

Introduction

Founded as a fortress on a virtually impregnable crag of volcanic rock, Edinburgh's first residents chose their site well. While they must have been exposed to the full brunt of the often biting winter winds, they enjoyed commanding views across the Lothians and Fife, and their strategic position helped to ensure their fledgling community not only survived the turmoil of the Middle Ages but also thrived. The burgh became Scotland's capital in 1437, and was the medieval equivalent of Manhattan, with tenements soaring several storeys high. Nearly six centuries later, Edinburgh is famed as one of the most beautiful cities in the world, a unique symbiosis of geography, geology and some truly inspired architecture.

Scotland's capital still reveals much of its long and fascinating history through its buildings, and both the Old and New Towns have been designated a UNESCO world heritage site. Indeed if it were possible for its medieval residents to see the city now, they would still recognise much of the Old Town, snaking its way down the natural ridge that connects Edinburgh Castle's crag with the Palace of Holyroodhouse, nestled at the foot of the dormant volcano known as Arthur's Seat. Some of the tenements on this so-called Royal Mile – made up of the four linked streets Castlehill, Lawnmarket, High Street and the Canongate – date back to the sixteenth century. People still worship at St Giles' Cathedral, drink in the old inns of the Grassmarket and bring in the New Year bells at the Tron Kirk.

To the north of the medieval heart of the old burgh, James Craig's New Town is no less remarkable. It fans out from Princes Street Gardens in symmetrical and spacious style, displaying its garden squares and crescents like jewels. These Georgian ideal homes not only make up one of the finest examples of urban planning anywhere in the world, they remain among Scotland's most sought-after residences. The city is liberally scattered with the post-Enlightenment landmarks that earned Edinburgh the epithet 'the Athens of the North', and while the smoke responsible for the city's other nickname might have cleared long ago, Auld Reekie's skyline is punctured by the Gothic spires of cathedrals, churches and the fantastical Scott Monument. The nineteenth century also saw many of the city's most iconic buildings erected – William Henry Playfair's the National Gallery and Royal Scottish Academy, the old Royal High School and Donaldson's College to name but a few. Even the unfinished National Monument, dubbed Edinburgh's disgrace, adds a touch of Grecian grandeur to Calton Hill.

There has been a long tradition of trying to preserve the city's built heritage but, as many of the photographs in this book clearly show, much of the old burgh has not survived. The Nor' Loch, which had formed a natural moat at the northern face of the Castle Rock, was drained to make way for Princes Street Gardens, and an artificial hill, The Mound, had to be built to help connect the Old and New Towns. Early nineteenth-century 'improvements' to the Old Town saw entire streets, such as St Mary's Wynd and part of the West Bow, disappear. High Street tenements were demolished to make way for North Bridge, and many others became so dilapidated that they could not be saved. It was only after a public outcry that the tenement known as John Knox's House, near the old Netherbow Port, was saved from demolition. The town council also intervened to save the Canongate's Huntly House, creating a museum of the city's history.

Today Edinburgh is much more than a carefully preserved museum piece, however. Whilst it has not escaped some scars of the brutalist architecture of the 1960s – the most notorious example is the St James Centre, now widely regarded as the city's ugliest building – there are some modern buildings of real quality. The award-winning Museum of Scotland has transformed the corner of Chambers Street, while the nearby Festival Theatre has breathed new life into the old Empire venue on the same site. An innovative underground link now connects the National Gallery of Scotland and the Royal Scottish Academy, opening into Princes Street Gardens. The heart of the Royal Mile has been enhanced by the Scottish Storytelling Centre, a modern building that connects with its centuries-old neighbours without descending into pastiche. Away from the city centre, the historic port of Leith has been virtually transformed following the decision to site the headquarters of the Scottish Government at Victoria Quay and its regeneration is ongoing.

In the past decade, one development has attracted more attention than all of these put together. In 2004, the Scottish Parliament building was officially opened at Holyrood, almost 300 years after the Act of Union saw Scotland governed from Westminster. Yet the early years of devolution were overshadowed by the controversy surrounding the construction of the parliament building, which was repeatedly delayed and spiralled to ten times the original estimated cost. Since the completion of the parliament, designed by the late Catalan architect Enric Miralles, its quirky style has won over many of its former detractors.

Further changes are now on the horizon. The old Royal Infirmary is at the centre of the Quartermile development, one of the largest regenerations ever seen in the city centre, while the proposed 'SoCo' project will aim to revive the Cowgate and South Bridge site ravaged by the 2002 fire that made headlines around the world. Perhaps most exciting of all is that the much-maligned St James Centre is set to be demolished and redeveloped, offering a once-in-a-generation opportunity to transform the east end of Princes Street and Leith Street.

With these exciting developments in prospect, Edinburgh looks set to continue its proud heritage of creating buildings that will inspire both residents and visitors for centuries to come.

EDINBURGH CASTLE FROM JOHNSTON TERRACE

One of the most imposing views of Edinburgh Castle

One of the most imposing, if not picturesque, views of Edinburgh Castle is from the south west vantage point. This image is dominated by the New Barracks, which were built into the castle's volcanic rock in the 1790s. The perimeter wall, complete with its rounded sentry boxes, was rebuilt by John Romer in the 1730s. The rather plain architecture and the sheer size of the five-storey barracks may not be pretty, but they are clear reminders of the castle's historic role as a fortress and military stronghold. Perhaps not surprisingly, this bulky addition to the castle was not universally liked. In 1859, proposals were put forward by Francis T. Dollman to renovate the barracks into a more ornate design resembling a French chateau. The designs were not adopted – evidently the Town Council preferred the more austere original. This undated photograph by Alexander Inglis has been taken from Johnston Terrace, which was built in the early nineteenth century as a new route into the Old Town.

Today the view of the castle from this vantage point is largely unchanged. Thanks to restrictions on high-rise developments in the city, the New Barracks are visible from several miles away. There have been some alterations, however. In the 1950s, railings were put up along the base of the Castle Rock to discourage children from climbing up the rock face. The rock itself has had to be strengthened after pieces of the volcanic crag began to crumble away. Johnston Terrace is not quite as useful a route into the Old Town as it might appear for motorists. The High Street was recently pedestrianised between the Lawnmarket and the junction with North Bridge and South Bridge. Parking is also increasingly at a premium in the city centre. However, it is a convenient spot for tour buses to park, particularly during the Military Tattoo.

OLD TOWN FROM EDINBURGH CASTLE

Looking on to Arthur's Seat and Salisbury Crags

Left: People have been enjoying this view for almost three thousand years – archaeological evidence of human settlement on the Castle Rock dates back to 900 BC. This undated photograph looks down from the castle over its Esplanade towards the Old Town, and the stunning natural backdrop of Arthur's Seat and Salisbury Crags in Holyrood Park (or the Queen's Park as it is also known). The small scale of the original Old Town is very clear from this vantage point – you can see almost down the length of the Royal Mile, from Castlehill to Holyrood, punctuated by the three spires of Tolbooth St John's Church, St Giles' Cathedral and the Tron Kirk. The foreground is dominated by the Half-Moon Battery itself, a defence built to protect the eastern side of this ancient stronghold after the so-called 'Lang Siege' of 1571–73. The battery was formerly armed by the Seven Sisters – seven bronze guns – long since replaced. Visible at the centre of the skyline is the distinctive dome of the Old College of the University of Edinburgh. Towards the right of the picture, partially obscured by the Half-Moon Battery, is the university's McEwan Hall at Bristo Square.

Above: This impressive vista is largely unchanged, thanks to ongoing efforts to protect the Old Town (which has been designated a World Heritage Site by UNESCO) from high-rise developments. The spires of Tolbooth St John's Church, St Giles' Cathedral and the Tron Kirk are still prominent though only St Giles' is still used by worshippers. St John's has been converted into The Hub, and is the headquarters for the Edinburgh Festival, while the Tron is a tourist attraction documenting the history of the Old Town. Edinburgh Castle has become one of Scotland's top attractions, with thousands of people visiting each year. While the 'then' photograph is not dated, it is clearly post-war as the Esplanade is set up to host the world-famous military Tattoo. The Tattoo first took place in 1949 and it remains one of the highlights of the Edinburgh Festival.

DUKE OF GORDON'S HOUSE

Home to the Keeper of Edinburgh Castle

The Duke of Gordon's House used to sit high on Castlehill at the top of the Royal Mile, though this image is taken from the rear vantage point of Johnston Terrace. The building is thought to date from the turn of the seventeenth century. The house is reputed to have been home to George, 1st Duke of Gordon, who was the Keeper of Edinburgh Castle. Gordon was tasked with defending the castle from attack by the Jacobite hero, 'Bonnie Dundee' – John Graham of Claverhouse, 1st Viscount of Dundee. Johnston Terrace itself was built in the nineteenth century, cutting across the gardens of Castlehill properties and connecting the Old Town with Castle Terrace. In Kay's Plan of Edinburgh, a map published in 1836, the street was called the 'New West Approach'. This photo was taken by Alexander Inglis in 1860.

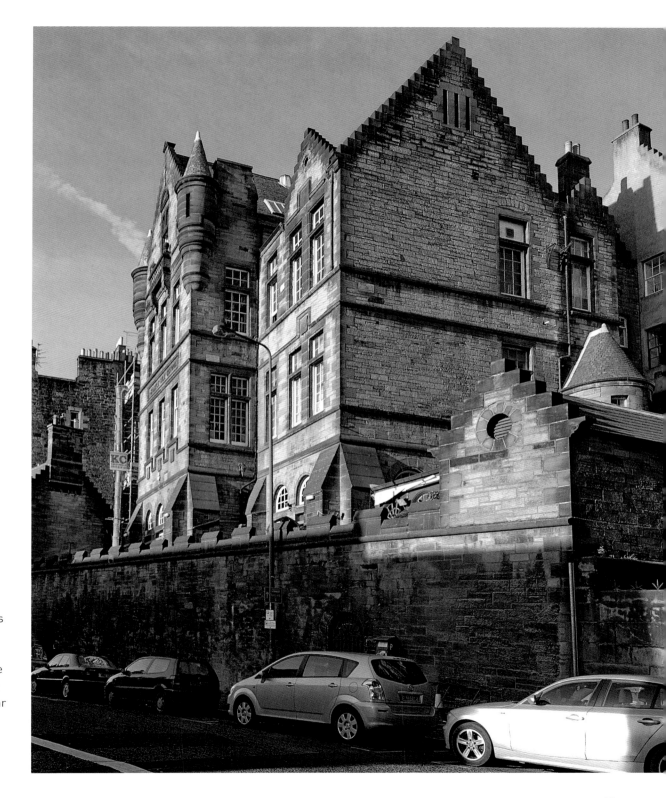

Around 30 years after Inglis took his photograph, the Duke of Gordon's House was demolished to make way for Castlehill Primary School. The school opened circa 1890, and its pupils certainly enjoyed one of the most beautiful locations in the city for their education. Following a decline in the number of families living in the Old Town, the school closed and the red sandstone building is now occupied by the Scotch Whisky Heritage Centre. This popular tourist attraction offers guided tours that reveal the whisky-making process and the differences between malt, grain and blended whiskies. The building also includes a bistro and bar in its basement where whisky lovers can enjoy tastings.

MILNE'S COURT

Built circa 1690 by Robert Mylne of Balfarg

Milne's – or Mylne's – Court was built around 1690, and was a significant development for the Old Town at the time of its construction. Robert Mylne of Balfarg, who was master mason to Charles II, demolished several 'closes' to create his court – three tenement blocks facing a courtyard. Given the overcrowding and lack of sanitation that families living in the Old Town must have endured, it probably represented a great improvement in their living conditions compared to their neighbours who were crammed into dark and cramped closes – conditions that would eventually prompt wealthier residents to fund the construction of the New Town from the 1760s. The development was one of those subsequently criticised by Patrick Geddes in his famous *Civic Survey of Edinburgh* of 1911, although this 1906 photograph shows that the Edwardian children living here had a reasonable amount of space and light to play in.

Today Milne's Court appears remarkably unchanged, though this photo belies substantial restoration work. The condition of the tenements deteriorated substantially after Geddes' survey and the buildings required reconstruction work during the 1960s, when they were converted into student residences. While Geddes may not have approved of their design, Milne's Court has doubtless retained sufficient character not to look out of keeping with the rest of the historic Royal Mile. If nothing else, the development remains of interest as an early attempt to improve the standard of living for ordinary Edinburgh people.

NORTH SIDE OF THE LAWNMARKET

Including Gladstone's Land, one of the best-preserved buildings in the Old Town

Left: The Lawnmarket is the site of one of the Old Town's main markets. Originally called the Land Market, as its traders sold produce from the land, this section of the Royal Mile runs from Castlehill to St Giles' Cathedral. This view of its north side, taken in the 1870s, includes one of the best-preserved buildings from the historic Old Town. Gladstone's Land, the tall merchant house in the centre of the picture, was completed in 1620 by the burgess Thomas Gledstanes. The plainer lines of the tenements to the left of Gladstone's Land are those of James Court, built in the 1720s and inspired by the open courtyard design of nearby Milne's Court. To the right of the picture is the entrance to Lady Stair's Close. The development of four-storey tenements was an attempt to clean up Old Town living conditions, with residents accustomed to slopping out into the street. James Court had some celebrated eighteenth-century residents – the philosopher and historian David Hume and the diarist and author James Boswell lived here. Yet the Victorian town planning visionary Patrick Geddes later branded such developments as 'Utilitarian blocks' that detracted from the unique character of the Old Town.

Above: The north side of the Lawnmarket is little changed since the Victorian age, and there have been significant efforts made to preserve its character. Gladstone's Land has been carefully restored, with the original arcade reinstated, to give visitors a taste of what life was like in seventeenth-century Edinburgh. Six rooms are furnished with period furniture and there is a painted ceiling that dates back to 1620. The building is now owned by the National Trust for Scotland, who believe it is the most important seventeenth-century tenement to survive in Edinburgh. Lady Stair's Close is now home to the Writers' Museum, a seventeenth-century house featuring exhibits on the works of Robert Burns, Robert Louis Stevenson and Sir Walter Scott. James Court remains largely in residential use.

SOUTH SIDE OF LAWNMARKET

Old Town tenements

Left: This photograph shows the tenements of the south side of the Lawnmarket in around 1911. The arched entrance near the coal-seller's cart leads into Brodie's Close – named after the father of the infamous Deacon Brodie, the gentleman robber whose double life is said to have inspired Robert Louis Stevenson to create the story of *Dr Jekyll and Mr Hyde*. The Lawnmarket was a busy shopping area and the stores here are selling their general wares to local people, many of whom were still resident in the Old Town tenements. As these tenements would have been overcrowded with little communal space for drying clothes, most people were using poles outside their windows to dry their laundry. The pawn shop at number 312 is perhaps an indication that the wealthier residents had moved to the New Town and other more salubrious areas of the city.

Right: Most of these tenement buildings have survived into the twenty-first century, though those to the far left, at the corner of George IV Bridge, were demolished in the 1960s to make way for the former Lothian Regional Council building. The council building was recently knocked down, however, and a hotel development was under construction at the time of writing. The old-fashioned shops have been largely replaced by those selling souvenirs to visiting tourists, with those selling cashmere and other woollen goods now the most popular outlets. Unlike the residents of 'Auld Reekie', modern Edinburghers have little need for either coal deliveries or clothes-drying poles.

TRAVERSE THEATRE CLUB, LAWNMARKET

One of the UK's leading theatres

The Traverse Theatre was founded as a theatre club at James Court, off the Lawnmarket, and it staged its first production in January 1963. The theatre was set up as a club in order to escape censorship and licensing laws, and it was also used as an exhibition space. This image, taken in 1966, shows the theatre's discreet sign outside James Court. The 60-seat theatre was housed in a former brothel known locally as 'Kelly's Paradise'. The theatre hit the local headlines shortly after it opened when actress Colette O'Neill was accidentally stabbed while playing a scene in a production of Jean Paul Sartre's play *Huis Clos*. After the James Court building became unsafe in 1969, The Traverse moved to a 100-seat venue in the West Bow, at the east end of the Grassmarket.

After the Traverse moved out, James Court returned to residential use, and this section of the Lawnmarket is now largely given over to retail outlets catering for the tourism industry that is now so important to the city's economy. Given its close proximity to the castle, this is one of the busiest stretches of the Royal Mile. Not everyone is happy with the proliferation of souvenir shops in the heart of a World Heritage Site, but the city council has little control over the type of business operating here. In 1992, the Traverse moved again, this time to Cambridge Street, just off Lothian Road and a stone's throw from both the Royal Lyceum Theatre and the Usher Hall. The new Traverse, designed by Nicholas Groves-Raines and costing £3.3 million to build, is part of the Saltire Court development that now dominates Castle Terrace.

VIEW OF CASTLEHILL, GEORGE IV BRIDGE AND LAWNMARKET

Dominated by the spire of Tolbooth St John's Church, now The Hub

Left: Taken from just outside the High Court on the Lawnmarket, this photograph looks up towards Castlehill and Edinburgh Castle itself. We can also see the junction with George IV Bridge, with the impressive Classical architecture of the Midlothian County Council building on the left. This purpose-built local government base was erected in 1900. Further up towards Castlehill, the dramatic 74-metre spire of the Tolbooth St John's Church dominates the picture. Designed by James Gillespie Graham, it was built in the early 1840s and served a dual purpose – as a church for the local congregation and as a meeting place for the General Assembly of the Church of Scotland. The General Assembly later moved to its current home at The Mound.

Above: The busy junction of George IV Bridge and the Lawnmarket has changed dramatically and is now undergoing further redevelopment. The corner tenements were demolished to make way for modernist offices built for the former Lothian Regional Council in the late 1960s. The building was used as a temporary administrative home for MSPs before the Scottish Parliament was built at Holyrood but it too was demolished and a new hotel development was under construction at the time of writing. By the early 1980s, St John's had fallen into disuse, but it was converted in 1999 into The Hub, the headquarters of the Edinburgh Festival, by the architect Benjamin Tindall. The former Midlothian County Council building became Lothian Region Chambers following local government reorganisation, but is now used as a registrar's office.

ST GILES' CATHEDRAL

First consecrated as St Giles' in 1243

Left: This undated image was probably taken after major restoration work was completed between 1872 and 1883. St Giles' – more correctly known as the High Kirk of Edinburgh – underwent major transformation in its earlier history. There has been a church on the site, near the Lawnmarket in the upper section of the Royal Mile, since the ninth century. It was first consecrated as St Giles' in 1243, by the Bishop of St Andrews. The church was a focal point during the Scottish Reformation, which saw Scotland's parliament break with the Roman Catholic Church in 1560 and forbid the celebration of mass. John Knox preached Presbyterianism from the pulpit here, famously railing against the arrival of the Catholic Mary Stewart to take up her throne as Queen of Scots in 1561. Riots broke out at the church in 1637 when Charles I tried to impose the *Book of Common Prayer*. It was around this time that St Giles' briefly became a cathedral, following the appointment of Scottish episcopal bishops.

Above: Visitors to St Giles' Cathedral will find it little changed since the Victorian image was captured. One of the most significant alterations came in 1911 when the Thistle Chapel, designed by architect Sir Robert Lorimer in a Gothic style, was added to the cathedral. A restoration programme that started in 1977 is still ongoing and has involved repairs to the church's roof and stonework and the installation of a new organ. In 1985, a new window was added, designed by the Icelandic artist Leifur Breidfjörd, that commemorates the poetry of Robert Burns. St Giles' remains the focal point for state occasions and national services of thanksgiving, as well as a place of worship for its congregation. An estimated 400,000 people visit the church each year.

MERCAT CROSS FROM PARLIAMENT SQUARE

Originally a meeting point for medieval traders and merchants

Left: Edinburgh's Mercat Cross (market cross) is shown here from Parliament Square, just off the High Street. The Mercat Cross was originally a meeting point for traders and merchants in the medieval burgh. It was also a place of entertainment – including the grisly spectator sport of watching public executions – and it marks the spot where royal proclamations were read out. The Mercat Cross shown here dates from 1885 and is at least the third version of the old burgh landmark. The first cross is known to have been in place further up the High Street during the early fourteenth century. It was moved by some burly Leith sailors in the seventeenth century when the street was widened. The former site of the cross is still marked out in the cobble stones near St Giles' Cathedral. The second cross was demolished in 1756, though the capital and parts of the shaft were preserved. They were erected on a new pedestal in 1866, and the unicorn finial was added. The sub-structure was built in 1885. According to research by the Royal Commission on the Ancient and Historical Monuments of Scotland, the carved capital at the top of the shaft dates back to the period 1400–1450.

Right: The Mercat Cross is no longer a focal point for traders, but it remains at the heart of the Old Town. In the main image, the cross is viewed from just inside Parliament Square, looking towards Parliament House, home to the Court of Session and the Faculty of Advocates. Parliament Hall, built in 1639 by Sir James Murray and home to the original Scottish Parliament until the Act of Union in 1707, still survives beyond the neo-classical facade. The inset shows the Mercat Cross from the same vantage point as the archive image. The vista is closed by the City Chambers building, which dates back to 1753 when it was the Royal Exchange and its piazza and arcade were designed for use by merchants. The north block is now used by the City of Edinburgh Council. It is the administrative headquarters for local government in the city, and the north elevation commands breathtaking views across the New Town towards Fife.

NEW ASSEMBLY CLOSE

This section of the High Street was substantially rebuilt after the Great Fire of 1824

Left: This image shows a couple heading into a production by the Unnamed Theatre Company at the Boogaloo Café, New Assembly Close, during the Edinburgh Festival in 1972. This address has a long association with the arts in the city. The name of the close refers to its former role as one of the various homes to the Assembly Rooms, before they moved to their current site at George Street in the 1780s. Robert Adam had designed a new building for them at the junction of South Bridge and Nicolson Street that would have kept the venue in the Old Town. This section of the High Street was substantially rebuilt after the Great Fire of 1824, which also destroyed part of the nearby Tron Kirk.

Above: Just through the archway is the Lord Reid Hall, originally built as a branch of the Commercial Bank in 1824. The hall later became the Edinburgh Wax Museum. The Edinburgh Wax Museum closed in 1989 and the Lord Reid Hall is now used by the Faculty of Advocates as a meeting room. This section of the High Street is one of the most vibrant in the Old Town, particularly during the Edinburgh Festival.

JOHN KNOX'S HOUSE

The reforming preacher was reputed to have lived here in the 1560s

Left: Whether John Knox ever lived at this location remains unclear, but this building has been long associated with the reforming preacher. He was reputed to have lived in the house in the 1560s – pictured in the centre of this 1880s photograph – when it was owned by the royal goldsmith James Mossman. Even if he didn't live there, tales of Knox preaching from the bow window of the house may still be true. However tenuous, Knox's link to the house almost certainly saved it from demolition by the Town Council. It was restored between 1853 and 1866, and by the time this photograph was taken, it appears to have become a tourist attraction. As the sign shows, the house was 'Open Daily from Ten till Four, Admission Sixpence'. Visitors looking for refreshment were also invited to stop at Knox's coffee house in Moubray House to the left, which dates back to the late fifteenth century and is probably the oldest surviving home in the city. To the right, we can see Knox's Free Church (later Moray-Knox Church), which was built in the 1850s as a memorial to the preacher.

Above: The major difference today is that Knox's Free Church has been demolished. It was knocked down in the 1960s and replaced by the Netherbow Arts Centre in the 1970s. The Netherbow itself is now the site of the Scottish Storytelling Centre, which is linked to John Knox's House. A carved effigy on the corner of Knox's House was thought to have been a likeness of the preacher. However, the image was recently confirmed as depicting Moses preaching the Ten Commandments. This section of the High Street is one of the busiest, with tourists frequenting a range of pubs of which it is doubtful that the Presbyterian Mr Knox would have approved.

MORAY-KNOX CHURCH / SCOTTISH STORYTELLING CENTRE

Knox Free Church opened in 1853 and later merged with the congregation of the Moray Church

The Moray-Knox Church was, as the name suggests, built in memory of John Knox, the leading light of the Scottish Reformation. Yet the construction of the church also helped to literally support the crumbling structure of his famous house. In 1839, the neighbouring Lord Balmerino's House collapsed, and during the 1840s Knox's house was in such a dilapidated state that the Town Council planned to demolish it. It was saved following the intervention of the Society of Antiquaries, renovated and turned into a museum. The building of the Knox Free Church next door helped to shore up the structure. The church was built after the congregation of the Canongate Free Church planned to raise £15,000 to erect two schools and two churches in memory of John Knox. Only the Knox Free Church was built, replacing the congregation's old meeting place on Macdowell Street, later renamed as New Street. It opened in 1853, and later merged with the congregation of the Moray Church.

The Moray-Knox Church was demolished in the 1960s and replaced by the Netherbow Arts Centre during the 1970s. The Netherbow Theatre became a popular venue for Edinburgh Festival shows. Following a £3.5-million redevelopment, The Netherbow was transformed into the Scottish Storytelling Centre. The storytelling centre, designed by Malcolm Fraser Architects, was completed in 2006 and is integrated with Knox's house. Unlike some other modern additions to the Old Town, which have been criticised as little more than poor pastiche of historical buildings, the award-winning design is refreshingly twenty-first century. There are some clever nods to the past, however. The forestair and tower – which provides a new home for the 1621 City Bell that once hung in the Netherbow Port – are clear echoes of Renaissance style.

MORAY HOUSE AND CANONGATE

Oliver Cromwell was reputed to have lodged here in 1648 and 1650

Left: Here the young children in the foreground of the photograph are entering the heart of the old burgh of Canongate, founded by the canons of Holyrood Abbey in the twelfth century. The Canongate, which stretches from the end of the High Street to the Palace of Holyroodhouse, takes its name from "canons' gait", or the way of the canons. To the left of the picture, we can see the Canongate Tolbooth (see page 36), but the image, taken around the turn of the last century, is dominated by Moray House on the right and its distinctive gateway, decorated with two obelisks. Dating from the early part of the sixteenth century, Moray House was built for the Countess of Home and then passed to her daughter, the Countess of Moray in 1643. Oliver Cromwell is reputed to have lodged here in 1648 and again in 1650. The stone balcony on curved brackets is a distinctive feature of the three-storey building, and is at the centre of

a gruesome story. The Marquis of Argyll is said to have stood on the balcony to watch his enemy, the royalist Marquis of Montrose, carted off to his execution at the Mercat Cross near St Giles' Cathedral. His exultation was somewhat short-lived, however, as Argyll himself was executed in 1661.

Above: By the middle of the nineteenth century, Moray House was being used for its modern purpose – for the training of teachers. The lodge house was added around this time. Moray House is now the main building in the Moray House School of Education, which is part of the University of Edinburgh. In the early part of the twentieth century, the Canongate had descended into slum conditions. Now it has been extensively restored and is once again a busy thoroughfare, not only for tourists but also for staff going to work at the nearby Scottish Parliament. The distinctive cobbles of the Canongate were recently replaced by ordinary tarmac, which has detracted from the character of the street, but doubtless improved the comfort of car and bus passengers alike.

ST JOHN STREET

Now dominated by Moray House College

Left: This undated image shows the St John's Land building and the adjoining tenements of St John Street, which connects the Canongate with Holyrood Road. To the centre of the picture, we can see the pend, or archway, which gives access to the Canongate. St John's Land was built in the 1760s by the Earl of Hopetoun and it was a sought-after address, albeit for a relatively short time, not least because the development was next to Moray House, famed for its fine gardens. According to Smollett, the best apartments were on the upper floors, which may well have been due to the fresher air, as the Earl's development still lacked proper sanitation. The extension of the city north into the New Town saw the better-off residents move out of the area, and the Canongate became one of the most impoverished and dilapidated parts of Edinburgh.

Above: By the 1950s, the St John's Land tenements had been acquired for Moray House College by the National Committee for the Training of Teachers. The St John's Land building was restored at a cost of around £41,000 and reopened in 1956. The exterior remains much the same, though the Georgian interior of the building was gutted to adapt it to the teaching needs of the college. St John Street's tenements have been demolished and the street is dominated by the extension of Moray House College, which is now part of Edinburgh University. The extension was supposed to have ten storeys, but the plans were revised following concerns that such a large development would not only spoil views of the Old Town skyline but also set a precedent for similar structures in the future. The Canongate area is once again in a state of transition following the closure of traditional breweries in the area and the recent opening of the Scottish Parliament building.

CANONGATE TOLBOOTH
The tolbooth dates back to 1591

One of the most distinctive buildings on the Royal Mile, the Canongate Tolbooth was the focal point of the old burgh before it merged with Edinburgh a little further up the hill. The building, which replaced a medieval ruin on the site, served several purposes: as a meeting place for its town council, as a court house and as a jail. The four-storey tolbooth, which features a tower complete with turrets and gun loops, dates back to 1591, although the clock was not added until the nineteenth century. To the right of the picture, the old Burgh Cross is visible, outside the entrance to Canongate Kirk. Like the Mercat Cross near St Giles' Cathedral, the Burgh Cross was the site for executions and proclamations. The cross dates from the sixteenth century, though its base, capital and crosshead were replaced in 1888. The kirk itself was built in 1688 on the orders of James VII, replacing the Abbey of the Holy Rood, which is in the grounds of the nearby Holyrood Palace. Its graveyard is the last resting place for economist Adam Smith and the poet Robert Fergusson.

Many visitors are surprised by how recently the Canongate became part of Edinburgh. The burgh of Canongate was acquired by its neighbour in 1639 but not formally merged with Edinburgh until 1856. Today the tolbooth is now used as a museum, The People's Story, which documents the lives of ordinary Edinburgh folk from the eighteenth century to the present day. As in the old picture, however, the Tolbooth retains a tavern – one of Edinburgh's several hundred pubs. One of the most recent and popular additions to the area has been a statue of the poet Robert Fergusson, who now strolls past the Canongate Kirk (far right).

HUNTLY HOUSE

Now the Museum of Edinburgh

Left: Sometimes called the 'Speaking House' in reference to the mottoes inscribed on its walls, Huntly House is one of the most famous buildings on the Canongate. The present construction dates from 1517 when James Acheson bought three small houses that were later joined together with a new facade closer to the street. It is unlikely that it was the town house of the Marquesses of Huntly, as its name suggests. The building was extensively altered in the late seventeenth century by the Incorporation of Hammermen, a trade organisation for metal workers including armourers, blacksmiths, clocksmiths, gold-and-silversmiths, locksmiths, pewterers and saddlers. By the early twentieth century, Huntly House was in a ruinous state and it was restored by Sir Frank Mears in the 1920s. It opened as a museum dedicated to the city's history in 1932.

Right: Huntly House was recently renamed the Museum of Edinburgh. Its treasures include Greyfriars Bobby's collar and feeding bowl (see page 118) and a window from the house of Baillie McMorran, a city magistrate shot dead by a schoolboy during a riot at the Royal High School in 1595. The panels now visible on the exterior of the building are copies of the originals. The Latin mottoes include: 'A well-balanced person takes the long term view', 'You decide what to say, I choose what to listen to' and 'Today it is me, tomorrow you; worrying achieves nothing'. The mottoes are echoed on the Canongate wall of the nearby Scottish Parliament building, which features 24 stones inscribed with quotations from psalms, proverbs and poetry by the likes of Hugh McDiarmid.

WHITE HORSE CLOSE

The seventeenth-century boarding point for stagecoaches to London

Left: White Horse Close dates back to at least the early seventeenth century, when a stabling inn was built there by Laurence Ord, though this is thought to have replaced an even earlier inn on the site. The close, which is near the foot of the Royal Mile, is reputed to have been named after the horse ridden by Mary, Queen of Scots, who chose to live in the nearby Palace of Holyroodhouse rather than Edinburgh Castle. Its proximity to the palace and to a nearby water supply made it a useful lodging place for nobility visiting the palace and a resting spot for thirsty horses. The close was also the starting point for passengers taking the stagecoach from Edinburgh to London. In the seventeenth century, the 400-mile journey which can now be completed in four or five hours by rail, would have taken more than a week. By the time this image was taken around 1900, transport had moved on, and the close was home to several poor families, with the buildings in a dilapidated state.

Above: Today White Horse Close remains a residential courtyard and in a far better condition than it was a century ago. Like much of the Old Town, it had fallen into a ruinous state by the early twentieth century, and the close required major renovation. A plaque at the site states that the construction dates from 1623 and that it was rebuilt in 1962. While the renovation incorporated sections of the original buildings, it is clear that there are noticeable changes, with the roof and staircase of the building on the right of the photograph significantly altered. The two-storey houses on the left no longer have a staircase, and the main building to the centre now features a crow-stepped gable.

PALACE OF HOLYROODHOUSE

The King James V towers were designed by John Ayton and added in 1528–32

Left: This undated image shows the entrance to the Palace of Holyroodhouse, viewed from Abbey Strand, at the foot of the Canongate. The King James V towers are in the centre of the photograph. The towers, which were designed by John Ayton, were added to the palace between 1528 and 1532. On the right, near the gates, we can see the remnants of the old gatehouse, including a stair tower, which was built by Walter Merlioun in 1502. Most of this old structure was demolished in the 1750s and incorporated into the Abbey Courthouse. Just to the left of the gates is the Abbey Sanctuary, where debtors sought protection from Holyrood Abbey. These cottages date back to the late fifteenth or early sixteenth centuries and were restored around 1916. The cottages and the adjacent tenement were bought by Lord Rosebery and given to the state in the 1930s.

Above: Although the cobbles have disappeared from the Canongate, and at the time of writing, the King James towers were undergoing restoration work, little has changed in this view of the palace today. The Abbey Sanctuary building has been preserved for future generations, though it is well over a century since anyone being pursued for debt has needed sanctuary here. To the right of the gates is the new Queen's Gallery, which was opened in 2002 as part of the Golden Jubilee Celebrations. The gallery was built in the shell of the former Holyrood Free Church and the Duchess of Gordon's School. The gallery shows exhibits from the Royal Collection and has enhanced the continuing allure of the palace as a popular tourist attraction. The fact that the Scottish Parliament building is a stone's throw away has brought even bigger crowds to this ancient part of Edinburgh.

PALACE OF HOLYROODHOUSE

This royal residence was originally founded in 1128 as an Augustinian monastery

Left: This splendid royal residence was originally founded in 1128 as an Augustinian monastery. According to legend, its name was inspired by King David I's vision in which a cross, or rood, appeared between the antlers of a stag. Kings often preferred to live in the relative comfort and shelter of Holyrood Abbey, rather than Edinburgh Castle on its exposed volcanic crag. The abbey now lies ruined and little of the original palace remains. The current building dates from 1501 during the reign of James IV. The palace was expanded during the reigns of James V and James VI, and substantially rebuilt at the behest of Charles II and to the design of the Scottish architect Sir William Bruce. The fountain was commissioned by Queen Victoria and designed by Robert Matheson in 1859. It was inspired by the seventeenth-century Cross Well at Linlithgow Palace. Despite its fairytale appearance, the palace was the setting for one of the bloodiest murders in Scottish history. Mary, Queen of Scots lived here between 1561 and 1567 and it was in her private apartments that her secretary, David Rizzio, was stabbed to death. This image shows Edwardian visitors enjoying the forecourt.

Above: Holyroodhouse Palace is not simply a tourist attraction for visitors intrigued by Mary, Queen of Scots – it remains a building fit for a queen. The palace is the current Queen's official residence in Scotland, and an annual summer garden party is one of the most prestigious events in the city. Ceremonies are also held at the palace to officially bestow honours to Scots who have been recognised in the Queen's New Year or Birthday Honours lists. Both photographs show the dramatic natural backdrop of Arthur's Seat and Salisbury Crags in Holyrood Park, also known as the Queen's Park.

HOLYROOD BREWERY / SCOTTISH PARLIAMENT

The new Scottish Parliament building was officially opened by the Queen in 2004

Above: Brewing was once a major industry in the Holyrood area, and the former headquarters for the Holyrood Brewery once dominated the corner of Horse Wynd, to the right, and Holyrood Road, to the left. This image was taken in 1989, a decade before the brewery was demolished to make way for the Scottish Parliament. The bland exterior of the building belies the fact that the brewery's roots dated back to 1749 when William Younger set up a brewery in Leith. William Younger II bought the Abbey brewhouse in Horse Wynd in 1803. Youngers later merged with McEwans to form Scottish Brewers, which became Scottish and Newcastle. In 1999 Scottish and Newcastle vacated the building and construction of the parliament began that summer. Ironically, Holyrood was actually not on the original shortlist for the parliament – it was initially proposed for sites near St Andrew's House at Regent Road, Victoria Quay in Leith or even Haymarket in the West End.

Right: If there is one corner of Edinburgh that has changed beyond recognition, it is the site of the Scottish Parliament. This view of the parliament building, designed by Enric Miralles, is from Horse Wynd. The bottom of Holyrood Road is now closed off, as the parliament building is integrated into Holyrood Park. Delays and spiralling costs dogged the project, which was finished three years late and hundreds of millions of pounds over budget. However, the quality of the finished design featuring motifs of leaves and upturned boats, has won over many of its former detractors. The building, which was officially opened by the Queen in October 2004, has become a popular tourist attraction. Sadly neither Enric Miralles nor the former First Minister Donald Dewar, who had championed a new-build parliament for Scotland, lived to see the building completed.

HOLYROOD BREWERY

The Holyrood Brewery was founded in the eighteenth century

The Holyrood Brewery was among a string in the area, thanks to a plentiful water supply which ran in a so-called 'charmed circle' from Fountainbridge in the west to the Canongate in the east. Following the Act of Union in 1707, Scottish brewers had the edge over rivals elsewhere in the country as there was no tax on malt north of the Border. During the Victorian age, Edinburgh became one of the largest brewing centres in the UK and exported beer all over the world. The Holyrood Brewery was founded in the eighteenth century, though much expanded and altered. The main building in this photograph of the Holyrood Road site dates from 1872, while the smaller building to the right was added in 1931 and designed by J.A. McWilliam. This image is undated but was taken in the 1970s, when an estimated 4,500 people were still employed by the brewing industry in Edinburgh.

Despite Edinburgh's long history of brewing, almost all the city's breweries have now closed. The Holyrood Brewery was closed by its owners, Scottish & Newcastle, in the late 1980s, and the site was redeveloped in the mid 1990s. Demolition of the old brewery buildings commenced well before the devolution referendum, let alone the announcement that the Scottish Parliament would be built nearby. While the main building was demolished to make way for housing, the slightly wider angle of this photograph shows the redevelopment of the 1931 building into a branch of the restaurant chain Pizza Express. Just out of shot to the right is the redeveloped Tun building, which is home to the BBC's Edinburgh base.

COWGATE AND ST MARY'S WYND

St Mary's Wynd was a main road into the heart of medieval Edinburgh

Left: St Mary's Wynd, just south of the High Street, was once a main road into the heart of medieval Edinburgh. St Mary's Wynd Port, or the Cowgate Port, at the junction with the Cowgate and the Pleasance, was a gateway in the Flodden Wall. St Mary's Wynd led up to the Netherbow Port, where the High Street meets the Canongate, and used to house St Mary's Chapel and a hospital. By the time this photograph was taken by J.G. Tunny, the Old Town thoroughfare had become an overcrowded and dirty slum. This image, taken in the 1850s, was shot before St Mary's Wynd was largely demolished and widened following the Improvement Act of 1867. The street was rebuilt between 1868 and 1869.

Above: Little now remains of the original St Mary's Wynd, which is virtually unrecognisable as today's St Mary's Street. The corner with the Cowgate, once the main route for bringing cattle for grazing, is now dominated by an unprepossessing budget hotel and car park. Much of the rest of the street retains some Victorian character, however. The recent regeneration of the Old Town and the opening of the Scottish Parliament have heralded improvements to St Mary's Street, with restaurants, boutiques and other specialist shops opening there. It remains a key route into the city centre from the south, and between the Old Town and New Town for motorists, as it links the Pleasance with Jeffrey Street.

COWGATE FROM SOUTH BRIDGE

South Bridge was built in the 1780s to help the city expand to the south

Taken from South Bridge, this 1958 image shows the Cowgate as it winds its way west towards George IV Bridge and the Grassmarket beyond. From this vantage point, it is possible to grasp the scale of the engineering projects undertaken to bridge the valley between the south side of Edinburgh and the high ridge of the High Street. South Bridge was built in the 1780s to help the city to expand to the south. It was designed by Robert Kay, although he had Robert Adam's earlier design to draw upon for inspiration. This image has been taken at the only point on the South Bridge viaduct where there is any significant gap between the buildings. The bridge was always intended to be lined with shops and other buildings, creating an illusion of walking at street level.

Fifty years on, the contrast is marked. On 7 December 2002, a fire took hold which destroyed a dozen properties in the Cowgate and South Bridge. While no one was injured, the damage to this part of the city's famous World Heritage Site made headlines around the world. The lost buildings included the popular Fringe venue, The Gilded Balloon, the Belle Angele nightclub and the University of Edinburgh's informatics department. Further devastation was only prevented by the swift actions of firefighters. This major gap site remains but probably not for long. Proposals have been drawn up by architect Allan Murray for a £40-million 'SoCo' redevelopment, including a hotel. If the plans are approved by the city's council, the development could be in place by 2011.

COWGATE FACING GEORGE IV BRIDGE

Including Magdalen Chapel, built in 1554

Taken from Cowgatehead at the eastern end of the Grassmarket, this undated image looks east down the Cowgate towards Magdalen Chapel and George IV Bridge. The bridge was built in 1832 to connect the Old Town and the south side of the city with the New Town to the north. It runs for around 300 metres, from Bank Street, near the top of The Mound, at the junction with the Lawnmarket to the corner of Chambers Street. Two Old Town streets – Liberton Wynd and Old Bank Close – had to be demolished to make way for the bridge. On the right of the picture, we can see the distinctive tower of Magdalen Chapel, an almshouse built in 1554, although its steeple was not added until the early seventeenth century. The initials of its benefactor, Michael MacQueen, a burgess of Edinburgh, and his wife, Janet Rhynd, are inscribed above the door.

Little has changed in this modern view of the Old Town thoroughfare. The tenements to the left of the picture have been demolished, but our perspective of the Cowgate remains much the same. Magdalen Chapel was renovated in the 1960s by George Hay and again in the late 1980s by Simpson and Brown. The chapel still features the only remaining intact examples of pre-Reformation stained-glass windows in Scotland. The Cowgate is now a busy thoroughfare, with traffic bypassing the High Street, which has been partially pedestrianised. A key route to the Scottish Parliament building at Holyrood, it is home to several nightclubs and bars and is very busy with revellers during the Edinburgh Festival.

WEST BOW FROM GRASSMARKET

Including the Bowfoot Well, built in 1674

Left: The West Bow once led up into the Old Town from the Grassmarket. Its zig-zag shape connected with the Upper Bow, a steep little street leading onto Castlehill. Between 1829 and 1834, during the city's improvements to the Old Town, the West Bow was partially demolished and closed off from the Upper Bow. Victoria Street and Victoria Terrace, designed by Thomas Hamilton, were added to connect the West Bow onto George IV Bridge. The Bowfoot Well, in the centre of this undated image, was part of a gravitational water system supplied by water from Comiston and designed by Sir William Bruce and George Sinclair. It was built by the King's master mason, Robert Mylne, and Peter Brauss in 1674, and repaired and altered in the 1860s.

Above: By the early twentieth century, like much of the rest of the Old Town, the West Bow and Victoria Street had descended into slum conditions. The West Bow is one of the best preserved parts of Edinburgh's Old Town. The west side of the street, to the left of the picture, retains several seventeenth- and eighteenth-century tenements. The red building with the distinctive curved gable is known as Crockett's Land and was built around 1705. The Bowfoot Well is no longer connected to the city's water supply, but was restored in the 1960s and scheduled as an ancient monument in 1970. The spire of the Tolbooth St John's Church, still towers above Victoria Terrace. Having retained much of its character, the West Bow is very popular with tourists, many of whom stop off for a drink at the Bow Bar, just out of shot, a traditional pub that is little changed since Edinburgh's heyday as a centre for brewing.

GRASSMARKET AND EDINBURGH CASTLE

A classic view of the castle atop its volcanic crag

Above: The dominant position of Edinburgh Castle atop its volcanic crag is particularly marked when viewed from the Grassmarket. From here, some of the oldest parts of the castle are prominent: the Half-Moon Battery on the left, the Palace and Great Hall on the right. This late Victorian image shows the Grassmarket in around 1880, when it was still very much at the heart of the hustle and bustle of the Old Town. It has been used as a marketplace since the fifteenth century, with a timber market and hay, or grass, sold for the city's cattle market. The Beehive Hotel in the centre of the picture is offering accommodation for carriers, while the lodgings at the Black Bull to the left are targeted at 'travellers and working men'.

Right: Many buildings in the Grassmarket have been restored and preserved. Apart from efforts to improve slum conditions, the historic marketplace was damaged during World War I when a German airship tried to bomb the castle. As a focal point for many tourists and revellers, the Grassmarket remains very much at the heart of the Old Town, though the inns that once catered for market traders are now more likely to be thronged with hen and stag parties. Many traditional pubs, including the Beehive (extreme left) and the Black Bull have survived. The green-painted White Hart Inn, which has given shelter to poets Burns and Wordsworth, dates from 1516. Hotels have sprung up on the south side of the Grassmarket and make a selling point of the spectacular views of the castle for wedding functions.

GRASSMARKET

This 1890s photograph shows the traditional All Hallows' Horse Fair

Taken in the 1890s, this photograph shows the traditional All Hallows' Horse Fair being held in the Grassmarket. The Hallow Fair was held at the beginning of November. As well as horse and other animal traders, it also attracted sellers of other goods, and apparently fortune-tellers. The event, according to the poet Robert Fergusson in his colourful poem 'Hallow-Fair', was 'whare browsters rare/Keep gude ale on the gantries/And dinna scrimp ye o' a skair/O' kebbucks frae their pantries.' The Grassmarket has also been used for a much more grisly purpose – the east end of the marketplace was the site of public executions until the late eighteenth century. A portable beheading machine called the 'Maiden' was often used.

While some of the buildings to the north side of the Grassmarket have survived, the tradition of All Hallows' Fair died out long ago. Regular markets had more or less stopped by the turn of the last century. In recent years, however, there have been efforts to revive the market tradition with special weekend events organised to sell French produce, for example. The wide public space has been dramatically reduced to make way for a road to connect the West Port to the Cowgate, and parking provisions have been made for motorists. In 1937, a memorial was erected at the east end of the marketplace, just out of this shot, to mark the spot where 95 Covenanters were executed between 1661 and 1668 during unrest over attempts to bring Scottish Protestantism in line with English Episcopalianism.

MEMORIAL TO DUGALD STEWART

A panoramic view of the East End from Calton Hill

Left: The foreground of this panoramic view of Edinburgh's East End, taken from Calton Hill, is dominated by the memorial to Dugald Stewart (1753–1828). Stewart was a professor of moral philosophy at Edinburgh University and this monument was designed by William Henry Playfair, inspired by the Choragic Monument of Lysicrates in Athens. To the left of the monument, we can see North Bridge, the spire of the Tolbooth St John's Church, the castle, the clock tower of the North British (now the Balmoral) Hotel, and the Scott Monument. To the right, we can look across the top of Leith Street towards St Andrew Square, the New Town and Corstorphine Hill in the distance.

Right: Few people today will know why Dugald Stewart was honoured by this impressive monument, but no doubt many will be impressed by Playfair's monument to him. The most dramatic difference in this part of the Edinburgh skyline is to the right of the monument, where the St James Centre, built in the late 1960s, has replaced St James Square and the top of Leith Street, virtually obliterating views of the New Town in the process. Today the views to the left of the monument remain remarkably unspoiled. The Scott Monument has a temporary neighbour – a ferris wheel erected as part of the Hogmanay street party entertainment.

EDINBURGH FROM CALTON HILL. J.PATRICK.

EDINBURGH SKYLINE
FROM CALTON HILL

Showing the thick smoke that gave Edinburgh its nickname of Auld Reekie

Left: The foreground is dominated by the Calton Gaol, which was designed by Archibald Elliot and built next to the Bridewell Prison by Robert Adam. Just beyond the old prison is the Calton Burial Ground. Here the obelisk monument to the Scottish Martyrs – based on Cleopatra's Needle in London – towers up towards the castle. This undated image has been taken after 1844, when both the obelisk memorial and the Scott Monument were erected but before the 1890s, when the stone North Bridge was replaced by a new steel version to accommodate the needs of Waverley Station. Construction of the North British Hotel on the corner of North Bridge and Princes Street had also yet to commence. The vista along Princes Street appears to be obscured by the thick smoke that gave Edinburgh its nickname of Auld Reekie.

Above: Most of the old Calton Gaol has gone, and while the Governor's House still survives, our view of it is now obscured by the north side of St Andrew's House, which dominates the foreground in Regent Road. St Andrew's House was designed by Thomas Tait and built between 1936 and 1939 to accommodate the Scottish Office. It is widely regarded as one of the most significant buildings to be constructed in Scotland in the 1930s. The building is now home to some departments of the devolved Scottish Government, though its main base is now at Victoria Quay in Leith. The clock tower of the Balmoral Hotel now partially obscures our view of the Scott Monument from this vantage point.

Few pupils could claim to have been educated in such a grandiose setting as the Royal High School, described as one of the finest buildings in Britain after its completion in 1829. The building has become an iconic landmark that has helped earn the city its epithet, the 'Athens of the North'. Indeed its design, by the architect Thomas Hamilton, was directly inspired by the Temple of Theseus in Athens. Eventually even Hamilton's design became too old-fashioned and the school moved away from Regent Road to new premises at Barnton on the outskirts of Edinburgh in 1968. This archive picture is undated but appears to pre-date motorised transport. The photographer appears to have caught the attention of the bearded gentleman near the centre.

OLD ROYAL HIGH SCHOOL

An iconic building that helped earn Edinburgh its epithet, the 'Athens of the North'

Earlier in the twentieth century, St Andrew's House – home to the former Scottish Office and now used by the Scottish Government – was built near the school. Its location led it to be considered as a base for a new Scottish Assembly, and it was even converted to include a debating chamber in the late 1970s and renamed New Parliament House. After the failed 1979 referendum the building lay empty and became a focal point for devolution campaigners. Even after the 'yes, yes' result in the 1997 referendum, the old school was rejected as a site for a new Scottish Parliament. The then Scottish Secretary Donald Dewar was in favour of a new building at Holyrood, possibly because of the Old Royal High School's connotations with the nationalist movement. The building is now owned by the city council and whilst it is occasionally used for events, its longer-term future remains unclear. It has been proposed as the home for a new Scottish National Photography Centre.

REGISTER HOUSE

One of Robert Adam's best-known buildings

One of Robert Adam's best-known buildings, the neoclassical Register House dominates this vista of the east end of Princes Street. At the time of its construction, Register House was the first major Scottish public building to be planned for decades, and it was hoped it would not only provide a fitting home for Scotland's national records but also stimulate further interest in the nascent New Town. Adam, who was architect of the King's Works, designed the building in 1772, and its foundation stone was laid two years later. Despite the fact that much of the ground was donated by the city, it is thought that the construction cost £40,000. The project was completed by Robert Reid in 1834. New Register House, designed by Robert Matheson, was added to the rear in the 1860s.

Register House is still home to many of Scotland's official records, looked after by the Government agency, the National Archives of Scotland. Historical and legal search rooms are now open to the public who want to look at government, court and church records or legal registers. The view of the Duke of Wellington's statue outside Register House is obscured by the traffic in the 1905 image, but both the statue and its double staircase can be clearly seen in this picture. The cobbles and tram lines have gone but this remains an extremely busy junction between North Bridge, Princes Street, Leith Street and Waterloo Place. The wide public space in front of Register House is often used by campaigners, street-sellers and buskers. The building now spares our views of the thoroughfare from being spoilt by the concrete bulk of the St James Centre at the top of Leith Street.

EAST END OF PRINCES STREET, LOOKING TO WATERLOO PLACE

This view is dominated by John Steell's statue of the Duke of Wellington

Left: This view of the east end of Princes Street, looking towards Waterloo Place, is fittingly dominated by the statue of the Duke of Wellington. The majestic bronze statue of the Iron Duke commemorates his famous victory in the Battle of Waterloo in 1815. John Steell's effort was thought to be one of the Duke's favourite memorials (he is said to have ordered two casts of it) and a fine example of equestrian sculpture, with much of its weight cleverly balanced through the horse's tail. But for the famous battle, Waterloo Place was supposed to have been called 'Regent Bridge'. It was designed by the architect Archibald Elliot as the gateway to Regent Road, which winds round the foot of Calton Hill. The thoroughfare bridges the gap over Low Calton and also served as a war memorial. To the far right of the picture, we can see the former General Post Office, built in the early 1860s.

Above: Very little has changed in the modern vista of the East End, other than the addition of modern street furniture such as traffic lights and bike racks. The Duke of Wellington still dominates this corner of Edinburgh's main thoroughfare, though it is treated with a little less respect than in his day – the statue's plinth is occasionally daubed with graffiti. The statue is close to Waverley Station, the city's main railway station, and is a convenient landmark for people meeting up in the city centre, though as the sparser crowds suggest, Princes Street has lost some of its allure for shoppers in recent years. After the General Post Office moved to more modern premises, it lay empty for several years but it was recently converted into the Waverley Gate office development.

PRINCES STREET
FROM SCOTT MONUMENT

The tower of Scott Monument gives panoramic views of the city and Calton Hill

Left: Victorians who climbed the Scott Monument would have enjoyed breathtaking views of the city, and particularly of Calton Hill with its growing array of monuments and memorials. From left to right on the hill, we can see the old Observatory, the Dugald Stewart Memorial, the National Monument and the Nelson Monument. The National Monument by Cockerell and Playfair, was built in the late 1820s as a memorial to the Scots who fell in the Napoleonic Wars. Lack of funds prevented the planned expansion. The unfinished memorial became an embarrassment to the city and was labelled 'Edinburgh's Disgrace'. This image has been taken between 1877 and 1896. The promenade and garden to the right of the foreground was erected in 1877, and the buildings immediately behind it, including the old North British Station Hotel, Cook's Tourist Office, and Dunlop's Hatters were demolished in 1896 and a new North British Railway Hotel was built on the site.

Above: The North British Railway Hotel may be called the Balmoral now but it continues to dominate the east end of Princes Street. By tradition, its clock runs a few minutes fast to help commuters who are rushing to catch their trains at Waverley Station. The hotel now partially obscures the Victorians' view of Calton Hill, but most of the columns of the National Monument are still visible. The monument is still often referred to locally as 'Edinburgh's Disgrace'. The Waverley Market was redeveloped in the mid-1980s into a shopping centre, initially also called Waverley Market but later renamed Princes Mall. Compared to the former promenade, the design of the modern shopping centre has effectively closed off much of this public space.

WAVERLEY BRIDGE

James Bell's iron bridge was built between 1870 and 1873

Left: Waverley Station first opened in 1846, built into the east end of the valley left between the Old and New Towns after the draining of the Nor' Loch. Taken from East Princes Street Gardens, this photograph shows Waverley Bridge in the early 1870s. The bridge was built by James Bell, the chief engineer of the North British Railway, between 1870 and 1873, and it replaced an earlier stone version. Bell's iron lattice bridge was rebuilt in the mid-1890s during extensive reconstruction of the train station, carried out between 1892 (after the opening of the Forth Bridge) and 1902. This was the second major overhaul of the station, which had also been rebuilt in the 1860s. At the end of the bridge, the Cockburn Hotel sits at the foot of Cockburn Street. The street was built in 1859–64 to improve access to the railway station from the Old Town. This S-shaped street joins the High Street near the Tron Kirk – its spire is visible to the left of the 'now' picture.

Above: As the main route into Edinburgh's principal railway station, Waverley Bridge is one of the busiest thoroughfares in the city. Several city bus tours, as well as the bus link to Edinburgh Airport, depart from Waverley Bridge. While Waverley Station is now category A-listed, its location – running underneath North Bridge towards Waverley Bridge – means it is not regarded as an iconic structure. Several architects have put forward ambitious proposals to remodel it and make the station fit for the twenty-first century. However, recent renovations of the station have been fairly modest in scale and have focused on improving access for passengers. Above Cockburn Street are the steep tenements of the High Street, while Market Street runs to the left of the Cockburn Hotel.

CASTLE AND PRINCES STREET FROM THE EAST END

A breathtaking view of some of Edinburgh's most famous landmarks

Left: This panoramic shot, taken from inside the North British Hotel, gives a breathtaking view of some of Edinburgh's most famous landmarks. The vista is dominated by Edinburgh Castle on the left and the Scott Monument to the right. In between, we can see the neoclassical grandeur of the National Gallery of Scotland and the Royal Scottish Academy at the foot of The Mound. Both were designed by Playfair and are among the most beautiful buildings in the city. In the foreground, buses are lined up on Waverley Bridge, though Princes Street itself is remarkably free of traffic, yet busy with shoppers. On the far right, we can see the city's most famous department store, Jenners, built in 1895 by William Hamilton Beattie. The six-storey shop was a replacement for an earlier store destroyed in a fire.

Above: Today this view is remarkably unchanged, though the vantage point is from the Balmoral Hotel – the new name for the North British – and has been taken from a different angle. In 2004, the National Gallery and Royal Scottish Academy were connected by the underground Weston Link, which opens unobtrusively into East Princes Street Gardens. Designed by architects John Miller and Partners, the new Link includes a lecture theatre, restaurant and education centre. Another major change has been the development of the Princes Mall shopping centre on the site of the old Waverley Market. The growth of out-of-town retail parks has seen Princes Street drop down the rankings of desirable shopping destinations, but Jenners is still an iconic store.

EAST PRINCES STREET GARDENS

Including the Bank of Scotland headquarters and the Free Church Assembly Hall

Left: The New Town splendour of East Princes Street Gardens also provides the ideal vantage point to view the Old Town skyline. High on the natural ridge that runs down from Edinburgh Castle, which is just out of shot to the right, are several notable buildings. The most prominent is the Bank of Scotland headquarters, designed by Robert Reid and Richard Crichton in 1801, and later expanded by David Bryce in the 1860s. To the right, with its twin square towers, is the Free Church Assembly Hall, designed by William Henry Playfair in the 1840s, and used for meetings of the Church of Scotland. In this undated image, several groups of men are relaxing on the gardens' putting green.

Above: The Bank of Scotland headquarters still looms large over the gardens, though it is no longer regarded as such a great icon for the city. The economic downturn of 2008 saw the UK Government approve the bank's merger with Lloyds TSB. The Church of Scotland's Assembly Hall was used as a temporary debating chamber for MSPs while they waited for the Scottish Parliament building to be completed at Holyrood. East Princes Street Gardens is now a focal point for the annual Hogmanay festivities – at the time of writing, it was being converted into a Winter Wonderland including an outdoor ice rink. Trains still run in the valley immediately behind the gardens before disappearing into a tunnel beneath The Mound.

PRINCES STREET
AT THE FOOT OF THE MOUND

With the Scott Memorial and the Royal Scottish Academy in the foreground

The Scott Monument towers above Princes Street in this photograph which was taken near the foot of The Mound, around 1903. The Binny sandstone of this 61-metre-high Gothic memorial to the novelist Sir Walter Scott, which was erected in the 1840s, looks relatively pristine, as does the newly built North British Hotel (to the left of the Scott Monument) which opened in 1902. The Royal Institution building dominates the right of the picture, taken around the time that it became the permanent home of the Royal Scottish Academy. Designed by Playfair, the Royal Institution was built in two phases in the 1820s and 1830s. It was initially home to the Royal Society, the Board of Manufactures and Fisheries and the Institution for the Encouragement of the Fine Arts. The statue of Queen Victoria, on top of the building, was carved by Sir John Steell.

Over the decades, the Scott Monument has had to be repaired several times. In the 1950s, loose pinnacles were repaired, and the monument survived storm damage in the 1960s. In the 1990s, the debate as to whether to clean the soot-blackened memorial was reignited. The City of Edinburgh Council commissioned a photogrammetric survey of the structure. It was decided not to clean the sandstone but a two-year restoration went ahead to replace any damaged pieces of stonework with Binny sandstone. The Royal Scottish Academy is now the leading exhibition space for living Scottish artists. Recently renovated, the RSA is now physically connected to the National Gallery by an underground link, which also opens into East Princes Street Gardens. At the time of writing, work was ongoing to prepare for the return of trams to Princes Street.

WEST PRINCES STREET GARDENS

Home to the National Gallery of Scotland, designed by William Henry Playfair

Left: The old Nor' Loch was drained to make way for Princes Street Gardens, providing a beautifully landscaped green space for the residents of the New Town. The gardens slope down from the edge of Princes Street into the valley beneath the Castle Rock. Here the gardens are clearly being enjoyed by crowds of local people, probably around the turn of the last century. The Mound, which provides the backdrop to this vista, was not part of the original New Town plans. However, as North Bridge and Lothian Road are almost a mile apart, it is not difficult to see why another route between the Old and the New Town was necessary. It started out as a muddy shortcut, encouraged by a Lawnmarket trader keen to lure customers from the New Town. The Town Council embraced the idea and some two million tons of earth left over from digging the foundations of the New Town were used to complete The Mound.

Above: Little has changed in Princes Street Gardens today, with visitors and locals alike still using the gardens to relax and unwind. The Ross Open Air Theatre is located in the west gardens, and is the focal point for the Hogmanay celebrations, though high winds have twice forced the cancellation of the fireworks display in recent years. Designed by Playfair, the National Gallery of Scotland, to the left of the picture, opened to the public in 1859. Along with the Royal Scottish Academy, it is now regarded as one of his finest buildings. The two buildings were designed to complement each other but with a contrasting design – the Gallery is built in the Ionic order while the RSA is in the Doric style.

EDINBURGH CASTLE
FROM CASTLE STREET

This view is dominated by the castle's military hospital

Left: This view of Edinburgh Castle, taken from Princes Street Gardens, is further evidence of the commanding position chosen when this formidable fortress was established. If the jagged edges of the basalt rock were not enough of a deterrent for any would-be attackers, this section of the castle is also protected by Dury's and Butt's batteries, built in the early eighteenth century. The photograph is dominated by the castle's military hospital, which was originally built as a powder magazine in the 1740s and then expanded in the 1750s. It was not converted into a hospital until the end of the nineteenth century, and it was used during World War I. This image was taken around 1909, probably on a Sunday judging by the number of walkers who are strolling at their leisure in the beautifully kept gardens.

Above: Although not the oldest part of Edinburgh Castle, the military hospital building is now recognised around the world. Part of the National War Museum, it provides the stunning backdrop for two annual firework displays which are among the highlights of the Edinburgh Festival and the Hogmanay party. Some of the most sought-after offices and hotel rooms in the city enjoy this view of the castle, which attracts more than a million visitors each year. In the foreground we can see the statue of the minister and philanthropist Dr Thomas Guthrie, erected in 1910. Guthrie campaigned for the education of poor children and the monument shows him with a ragged boy. At the time of writing, Princes Street was undergoing work to prepare for the reintroduction of trams.

WEST END OF PRINCES STREET

Decorated to celebrate the visit of King George V and Queen Mary in 1911

Left: Here the west end of Princes Street is lavishly decorated to celebrate the visit of King George V and Queen Mary in 1911. It was a belated coronation party as he had been crowned king in 1910, following the death of Edward VII. The organisers were clearly expecting crowds as a stand has been built towards the left of the picture. The royal couple visited the Royal Infirmary whilst in the city, and to commemorate the event, Ward 7 was renamed the King George V Ward and Ward 30 the Queen Mary Ward. The Queen visited the hospital again in 1920 and the couple both visited the Princess Elizabeth Nursery in 1933. George V reigned until 1936 and was succeeded by his son Edward VIII who of course was never crowned king because he abdicated in order to marry the American divorcee Wallace Simpson. We can see that motorised transport had arrived in the city by this point, though most people would have depended upon trams.

Above: While royal visits are a rarity, the west end of Princes Street remains one of the busiest shopping and commercial districts of the city. Without the decorations to block our view, we can see the Caledonian Hilton Hotel (behind St John's Episcopal Church on the left), the Rutland Hotel (centre), and Shandwick Place (right). Transport is a key issue for this part of the city centre. Trams were discontinued in November 1956 to make more room in Edinburgh's narrow streets for cars. Ironically trams are now scheduled to return to the city in a bid to persuade motorists to reduce their car use. The first phase of tram development, which will connect Edinburgh Airport with Newhaven via Princes Street, is due for completion in 2011.

WEST END FROM THE RUTLAND HOTEL

With the Scott Monument, the North British Hotel and Nelson's Monument on the horizon

Left: This view of Princes Street, crowded with shoppers, was taken about 1903, from the site of what is now the Rutland Hotel at the west end of Shandwick Place. We can see that transport was at something of a crossroads – while some horse-drawn carriages and carts are still on the road, cable car trams are in operation. The first motorised bus was introduced in 1906. The right of the picture is dominated by the St John the Evangelist Scottish Episcopal Church, at the corner of Lothian Road. Built by William Burn between 1816 and 1818 on the site of a market garden, it prompted the owners of property on the north side of the street to lobby for legislation to prevent further development that might block views of the castle. The vista includes the spire of the Scott Monument, the clock tower of the North British Hotel, and Nelson's Monument on Calton Hill.

Above: Most of the changes to this part of Princes Street in the last century have been cosmetic. Traffic lights and islands have certainly cluttered the road space, and the old-fashioned awnings have been removed from the shops, making their displays more visible to passengers on the top decks of the many buses that run along Princes Street. Most of Princes Street is now closed to cars, but congestion is still a problem at this busy junction with Lothian Road. St John's Episcopal Church is still used by worshippers, and in recent years, the wall facing onto Princes Street has been used to display striking murals with messages on peace and justice. Just out of shot to the left is the House of Fraser department store, formerly known as Binns, which is a popular meeting point.

PRINCES STREET AND NEW TOWN FROM EDINBURGH CASTLE

This panoramic view takes in Leith, the Firth of Forth and Fife

Left: Taken from Edinburgh Castle, this panoramic view of the city takes in Princes Street, the New Town, Leith and beyond the Firth of Forth to Fife. In the foreground we can see the grand scale of West Princes Street Gardens, with the tiered seat of the Ross Bandstand towards the bottom left of the picture. By the 1950s, concerns had been growing about the future direction of Princes Street, and the Princes Street Panel was established to regulate its development. Far right in this picture is the 1966 New Club building designed by Alan Reiach, with shops at street level and a walkway at the first floor level. The original plan was for a continuous walkway along the entire length of Princes Street but the redevelopment was abandoned by the late 1970s.

Above: Although landscaping in the gardens has added more trees, our view from the castle today is largely unchanged. More than 40 years after Reiach's attempt to modernise the street, concerns about the future of this flagship shopping destination persist. The growth of out-of-town retail parks, parking restrictions and out-dated retail units have seen Princes Street drop down the rankings of major shopping destinations. Recent efforts to upgrade the historic thoroughfare have met with mixed fortunes, partly because so many different owners and lease-holders would need to join forces if the street's so-called 'rotten teeth' were to be pulled.

GEORGE STREET

The central thoroughfare in James Craig's New Town plan

Named after King George III, George Street was the central thoroughfare in James Craig's New Town plan. Here George Street is viewed from the junction with Castle Street, looking towards St Andrew Square in the east. Wider than either Princes Street, which runs parallel to the south or Queen Street to the north, George Street was originally a grand residential thoroughfare. The statue to the left of the picture is of Dr Thomas Chalmers, a Church of Scotland minister who led the 'disruption' of the church and sparked the formation of the Free Church of Scotland. The bronze memorial was sculpted by Sir John Steell in 1878, and shows Dr Chalmers dressed as Moderator of the General Assembly. The plinth is made of red granite.

By the 1980s, George Street was largely given over to banks, building societies and offices with a few specialist retail outlets. In the past decade, however, the street has undergone something of a renaissance. While Princes Street has seen its fortunes decline, with budget stores and souvenir shops moving in, George Street has been promoted as the 'Bond Street of the North'. High-end retailers and boutiques now line the street, and several former bank buildings have been converted into stylish restaurants and bars, including The Dome and The Standing Order. Much of the street's original Georgian architecture has been preserved, though the tenement building on the corner of Castle Street, behind the statue of Chalmers, has been replaced by a modern office and retail development.

ST ANDREW SQUARE

With the Melville Monument, built in memory of Henry Dundas, 1st Viscount Melville

Left: St Andrew Square marked the eastern end of James Craig's original New Town. In this undated image it is dominated by the Melville Monument, built in memory of Henry Dundas, 1st Viscount Melville, a former First Lord of the Admiralty. The memorial was commissioned by a group of naval officers who had raised some £3,500 for the project. It was designed by the architect William Burn and inspired by Trajan's Column in Rome. The column is 41 metres high and lighthouse builder Robert Stevenson helped to ensure that the foundations could cope with its weight. The statue itself was designed by Francis Chantrey and carved by stonemason Robert Forrest in 1837. The monument was originally supposed to be erected at Melville Crescent in the West End and became the subject of a court battle. The elaborate monument in the foreground was erected as a memorial to Gladstone in 1917, and was actually in the middle of the road, at the junction with George Street. By the 1950s, it was deemed a traffic hazard for double decker buses and it was moved to Coates Crescent in the west end at a cost of £3,000.

Right: Today St Andrew Square is at the heart of Edinburgh's financial district, with branches and offices of the Royal Bank of Scotland and Halifax Bank of Scotland. Recently the St Andrew Square Bus Station – the main station for services going to towns and cities outside Edinburgh – was revamped and a new shopping street, Multrees Walk, now connects the square with the St James Centre. The exclusive department store, Harvey Nichols, has opened a flagship outlet on the corner of Multrees Walk and St Andrew Square. Like most New Town gardens, St Andrew Square's garden was restricted for residents' use, but the square was recently opened up to pedestrians, creating a new public space in the city centre. The removal of the Gladstone memorial has also opened up views of the eastern side of the square, including the British Linen Bank building.

BRITISH LINEN BANK, ST ANDREW SQUARE

Designed by David Bryce, it cost £30,000 to build and was completed in 1851

Left: One of the most ornate bank buildings in the city, the British Linen Bank was a grand design even by contemporary standards. Designed by David Bryce as a replacement for the bank's headquarters on an adjacent site at St Andrew Square, it cost an estimated £30,000 to build and was completed in 1851. The structure dwarfs the building to the left of the picture, despite the fact that both only have three storeys. Six huge Corinthian columns run between the two upper floors and a parapet that supports six statues. The statues represent Agriculture, Art, Science, Manufacture, Commerce and Navigation, and were designed by Alexander Handyside Ritchie.

Above: The building is remarkably well-preserved and is now home to a branch of Halifax Bank of Scotland. With the advent of online and phone banking, such buildings have been increasingly expensive to maintain. The former British Linen Bank is one of the few banks in the New Town to have survived conversion into another use. In nearby George Street, several former banks have been converted into bars, including The Dome and The Standing Order. Following recent economic turmoil, which has seen Edinburgh's reputation as a major financial centre thrown into doubt, we should perhaps expect more of these majestic buildings to have only an historical link to banking.

CHARLOTTE SQUARE

Designed by Robert Adam, it is the jewel of Edinburgh's New Town

Left: Designed by Robert Adam, Charlotte Square was built at the western end of James Craig's New Town. From the start, it was intended to be home to some of the wealthiest citizens in Edinburgh, as the beautiful neoclassical facade of this section of the square suggests. This view of the northern side of the square shows its palatial frontage of the three-storey houses, which also have a basement below street level and an attic. The centrepiece is No. 6, which was built around 1796 and sold to Sir John Sinclair in 1806. It was revamped for the Marquis of Bute in 1905, and in 1966 it was acquired by the state for use as an official residence by the Secretary of State for Scotland.

Above: Charlotte Square is probably the jewel of Edinburgh's New Town, and it is now regarded as one of the most important urban developments of the eighteenth century. Most of the Charlotte Square houses are now used as offices, but No. 7, the Georgian House, is now owned by the National Trust for Scotland. The basement, ground and first floors have been painstakingly restored to resemble their original eighteenth-century glory, and the stark contrast of life below and above stairs. The Georgian House has become a popular tourist attraction, and its drawing room can also be hired for weddings and other events. Since the Scottish Parliament was established in 1999, No. 6, Bute House, has been used as the First Minister's official residence.

SIR WALTER SCOTT'S HOUSE,
NORTH CASTLE STREET

One of the best-preserved parts of James Craig's original New Town plan

Left: Castle Street runs from Queen Street in the north to Princes Street in the south of James Craig's original New Town grid plan. Like the rest of the New Town, Castle Street's tenements and houses were built to attract the upper classes. The street's most famous resident was Sir Walter Scott, the novelist and lawyer, who lived at No. 39 from 1802 until 1826. Scott's home is part of a three-door tenement block designed by Robert Wright and James McKain to look like a mansion house. The building (inset) has a distinctive double-bow front and can be seen on the left-hand side of the street in the main photograph. The vista looks uphill towards the junction with George Street and through the haze of smoke, beyond the statue of Lord Melville, we can just make out Edinburgh Castle.

Above: The north section of Castle Street – on some maps referred to as North Castle Street – is now one of the best-preserved parts of Craig's New Town, though the tenement on the left corner of George Street has since been demolished and rebuilt. The street has benefited from the regeneration of nearby George Street, with its style bars and high-end boutiques. The southern part of Castle Street, near Princes Street, has been pedestrianised and is regularly used as a marketplace. Until recently, Sir Walter Scott's House was home to Edinburgh lawyers Murray Beith Murray. In September 2008, however, the firm moved to new premises at Glenfinlas Street after it became increasingly difficult to use the Georgian property as a modern office.

MELVILLE CRESCENT

The statue of Viscount Melville was sculpted by John Steell in 1857

Melville Street was built as part of the West End phase of the New Town, designed by Robert Brown in 1813. Melville Crescent sits in the middle of the street, but it was not part of the original plans for the development, and would not have existed without a legal wrangle over where to put a statue. The story, reported in the famous 1823 case, Walker v Melville, began when a group of naval officers wanted to erect a monument to Lord Melville, First Lord of the Admiralty and were scouring the city centre for a site where it could be visible from the sea. Land owner William Walker changed his development plans to clear a space for the monument, creating Melville Crescent. When the officers decided to erect the monument at St Andrew Square instead, Walker sued. Having cleared the space, another statue was put at the centre of the crescent. It is of Melville's son, Robert, Viscount Melville and was sculpted by John Steell in 1857.

Melville Crescent is little changed since the days when Walker sought compensation for the loss of the Melville Monument. Few local people are now aware of the statue's story. Like much of the New Town, this area of the West End has been largely given over to office and commercial use and is the base for many legal and accountancy firms. The unusual width of the road here has enabled the city council to use Melville Street when diverting traffic away from Shandwick Place during recent work to prepare for the reintroduction of trams. Much of the traditional cobbled surface has been replaced with ordinary tarmac.

LOOKING WEST FROM EDINBURGH CASTLE

Showing the West End of the city to Corstorphine Hill

As visitors to Edinburgh Castle quickly discover, this ancient stronghold is a collection of buildings, added and much altered over the centuries, rather than a single structure. Here we can see the Governor's House on the left, with the old cart sheds and the former military hospital on the right. From this vantage point on the Castle Rock, the West End of the city stretches out towards Corstorphine Hill. In the centre, we can see the Caledonian Hotel, the grand former station hotel which dominates the foot of Lothian Road as it joins Princes Street. (Its distinctive red sandstone is visible in the 'now' image.) Just to the rear of the hotel is the Venetian-style campanile of St George's West Free Church on Shandwick Place. The church was built in 1866, but its impressive 56-metre-tall campanile-style bell tower, designed by R. Rowand Anderson, was added in 1881. To the left of centre are the three towers of St Mary's Cathedral at Palmerston Place, designed by Sir George Gilbert Scott and built in 1873–79, with the western towers added between 1914 and 1916.

No modern high-rise developments have marred this spectacular view of the city's skyline. The spires of St George's and St Mary's churches are still clearly visible, as is the six-storey 'Caley' Hotel (now the Caledonian Hilton), which remains one of the best-known places to stay in Edinburgh. However, the Caledonian train station, also known as Princes Street Station, that the hotel would have initially relied on for much of its business closed long ago and was demolished in the late 1960s. On the Castle Rock itself, the Governor's House is now used as an officers' mess, as the post of Governor was abolished in 1860. The former military hospital, which was requisitioned during World War I, is now part of the National War Museum of Scotland. The old cart sheds are now used as a café, with picnic tables set outside for visitors to relax and enjoy the impressive views.

Designed by Murray and Pilkington, the Synod Hall was built in Castle Terrace in 1875, originally as a theatre and then used by the United Presbyterian Church from 1877. It later reverted to an entertainment venue, becoming Poole's Diorama in 1906 and a cinema in 1928. The venue closed in October 1965. This photograph from the archives of *The Scotsman* newspaper shows its demolition taking place during the spring of 1966. The vantage point is near where Castle Terrace meets Spittal Street, in order to show the castle in the background. The site, which is close to the Usher Hall and Royal Lyceum Theatre, was earmarked for a new opera house. Following the demolition work, plans for an opera house stalled and the area became notorious as 'the hole in the ground'.

CASTLE TERRACE

Site of Synod Hall, now Saltire Court

After languishing for more than 20 years, the gap site in Castle Terrace has undergone a transformation. The 'hole in the ground' has been filled by the massive Saltire Court office and theatre development, which takes up the block between Cambridge and Cornwall streets. The three-storey building with an attic level and central atrium, was designed by Campbell and Arnott and completed in 1991. The building features red sandstone towers at each end – echoing the design of the Synod Hall. Saltire Court is now a base for lawyers' offices, including the leading firm Dundas and Wilson. The western end of the building is occupied by the Traverse Theatre, designed by Nicholas Groves-Raines.

ABC CINEMA,
LOTHIAN ROAD

The first cinema in Europe to convert its single screen into three auditoria

Left: This corner of Lothian Road used to be home to Port Hopetoun, at the end of the Union Canal. After the port was abandoned in 1922, and drained shortly afterwards, the site was redeveloped in the 1930s, creating a single building, Lothian House, which runs for a whole block from Morrison Street to Fountainbridge. The Morrison Street corner of the Art Deco structure, which features distinctive iron panelled detailing around the windows, became home to the ABC Theatre in 1938. By the 1960s, the ABC was a leading cinema and also one of the most popular music venues in the city – The Beatles and a host of other stars including Gene Pitney, the Walker Brothers and Herman's Hermits played here. When this photograph from *The Scotsman*'s archives was taken in 1969, the ABC was the first cinema in Europe to have converted its single screen into three auditoria. *Goodbye Mr Chips*, *Ice Station Zebra* and *Moon Zero Two* were all showing.

Above: Like many cinemas, the ABC, which was also later known as the Cannon, struggled to cope with competition from modern multiplexes and the advent of video. The cinema closed in 2000, and apart from the Art Deco facade, it was demolished in early 2001. The site was redeveloped as a cinema, however. In September 2003, after closing their theatre at Clerk Street in the south side of the city, the Odeon moved in. The new cinema features a four-screen 'miniplex', and the plush modern interior is designed to recreate the feeling that going to the cinema should be an experience. Unfortunately, its former home at Clerk Street remains closed and has been added to the Buildings at Risk Register. The stretch from Lothian Road to Leven Street, just past Tollcross, now boasts three theatres and three cinemas, as well as the concert venue Usher Hall.

OLD ROYAL INFIRMARY

Designed by David Bryce and completed in 1879

This impressive clock tower was the focal point of the former Royal Infirmary of Edinburgh at Lauriston Place. Designed by the architect David Bryce, this Scotch baronial building opened in October 1879 as a replacement for the eighteenth-century infirmary designed by William Adam. Following the advice of nursing pioneer Florence Nightingale, the new hospital featured a pavilion design, which allowed staff to isolate wards more easily in order to prevent the spread of infection. The height of the 41-metre clock tower was perhaps not quite so practical, however. In this photograph, taken around 1910, the hospital had borrowed a ladder from a nearby fire station to clean the clock face.

The Royal Infirmary moved to a new-build site at Little France, on the outskirts of Edinburgh, in 2003. Many local people continue to have fond memories of the Lauriston Place site, however, not least because so many people were born at its Simpson Memorial Maternity Pavilion. At the time of writing, the old infirmary was being converted into the Quartermile residential and commercial property development. Quartermile will feature 900 apartments, plus 30,000 square metres of office space and 10,000 square metres of retail and leisure space, all set in seven acres of green space. According to the architects, Foster & Partners, the idea is to 'roll The Meadows back into the city'. The development has already received several awards, including an award for Best Regeneration from the Royal Institute of Chartered Surveyors in Scotland.

OLD COLLEGE,
UNIVERSITY OF EDINBURGH

The university's most iconic building

Left: One of Scotland's oldest and most prestigious seats of learning, the University of Edinburgh's headquarters were purpose-built in the nineteenth century. The careful symmetry of the design of the Old College belies its somewhat troubled inception, however. The building was originally conceived by Robert Adam, the architect responsible for much of the neoclassical beauty of the New Town. Work began in 1789, but Adam died in 1792 before he could finish the project. Following the outbreak of war with Napoleon's France, the partially completed building lay derelict, and it would take decades to finish. William Henry Playfair won a competition to replace Adam, and his revised design departed significantly from Adam's original plans, which had envisaged two courtyards. The costs may have been a factor, however, as funding shortages repeatedly delayed the completion of the building. In fact, it was only finished after Parliament agreed to bail out the project to the tune of £10,000 a year. The scale was certainly ambitious. Six massive pillars at the entrance to the college on South Bridge were hewn from single blocks of sandstone. Each pillar weighed around nine tons and had to be brought from the quarry at Craigleith in special carriages pulled by 16 horses.

Above: While the university still has its administrative headquarters and some of its teaching departments, including its Faculty of Law, at this impressive base, its campus is very much integrated with the rest of Edinburgh. During the twentieth and twenty-first centuries, the university has expanded to sites across the city, most significantly at its 'science colony' at King's Buildings, West Mains, near the city's observatory, and at George Square. The university's medical school recently began relocating from Teviot Place to new premises at the Chancellor's Building adjacent to the new Royal Infirmary of Edinburgh at Little France. However, Old College remains the university's most iconic building and there is a plethora of cafés, bars and bookshops in the surrounding areas of South Bridge, Chambers Street and George IV Bridge.

GEORGE SQUARE

Built in 1766, the square was a forerunner to the New Town

Left: When it was built in 1766, George Square, just south of the Old Town, was a forerunner to the New Town. It was designed by the architect James Brown, and whilst its spacious three-storey houses would have been luxurious compared to the cramped conditions of the Old Town, wealthier residents would have preferred the more fashionable New Town, with its amenities like Princes Street Gardens and the Assembly Rooms at George Street. By the 1940s, the square was earmarked for the extension of the University of Edinburgh. The redevelopment of George Square was drawn up by Charles Holden in 1947, and Sir Basil Spence was brought in as a planning consultant. Two centuries after it was built, George Square was partially demolished. This photograph from the archives of *The Scotsman* newspaper, taken in 1955, shows the demolition work in progress.

Above: Only the east and part of the west side of Brown's original square now survives, and it is dominated by the university's 1960s redevelopment. This photograph shows the Hugh Robson Building, named after the university's principal between 1974 and 1979. Other buildings at George Square include the 14-storey David Hume Tower, the Adam Ferguson building, the Main Library and the George Square Theatre. The theatre is often used as a venue during the Edinburgh Festival and in recent years the garden in the centre of the square has been opened up for the Spiegeltent, the world-famous travelling 'tent of mirrors'.

CHAMBERS STREET
AND GEORGE IV BRIDGE

Now dominated by the Museum of Scotland

Left: This 1908 image shows the corner of Chambers Street and George IV Bridge, near the Old Town. Towards the right of the picture, we can see the North Free Church. The church was built by Thomas Hamilton and opened in 1846. It was constructed on the site of the former Edinburgh Bedlam, the asylum where the poet Robert Fergusson died. Its decorated design is not thought to have pleased its congregation, however, as they are reported to have described it as 'ugly and inconvenient'. The wide domed roof of the University of Edinburgh's McEwan Hall is just visible to the left of the church in the picture. The hall opened in 1897 as a venue for graduations and was designed by Sir Robert Rowand Anderson.

Above: This vista has changed dramatically, with the site now dominated by the Museum of Scotland, which was completed in 1990. Many might think it has changed for the better, with some unremarkable shops and tenements replaced by a building of real quality. With its drum tower and angled walls, Benson and Forsyth's award-winning design has been much praised. The Royal Fine Art Commission for Scotland described it as a 'worthy building' for the city and strongly recommended that the design be granted planning permission. The North Free Church is still intact, though it has long fallen out of use as a meeting place for worshippers. It is now the Bedlam Theatre, and a popular venue in the Edinburgh Fringe. The McEwan Hall is still used for university graduations.

GREYFRIARS BOBBY

The faithful terrier who guarded his master's grave for 14 years

Left: 'Greyfriars' Bobby is now world-famous as the faithful terrier who stood sentinel at his master's grave for 14 years. Eleanor Atkinson's novel *Greyfriars Bobby* published in 1912 documents Bobby's devotion to his master, John Gray, a Borders shepherd who died in 1858. Bobby continued his vigil at the graveside in Greyfriars Kirkyard, relying upon the kindness of local people, including John Traill (pictured inset), the owner of nearby Traill's Coffee House, to feed him. After Bobby's own death in 1872, he was buried beside his master. In 1873, this memorial was unveiled at the behest of Baroness Angela Burdett-Coutts at the junction of George IV Bridge and Candlemaker Row, a stone's throw from Greyfriars. The main plaque pays tribute to the 'affectionate fidelity' of the dog who 'followed the remains of his master to Greyfriar's Churchyard and lingered near the spot until his death in 1872'. Designed by William Brodie, the bronze statue and granite column incorporated both a drinking fountain and an octagonal water trough for dogs. In the main image, taken by A.A. Inglis in 1905, its fountain was still working – indeed a little dog has stopped by for a drink.

Right: The water supply to the drinking fountain may have been turned off in 1957, but the memorial remains a favourite spot for visitors to the city, and particularly for local children who are still inspired by the story. Despite his enduring popularity, however, Bobby has occasionally fallen victim to attacks and accidents. Bobby was stolen by Edinburgh University students in 1959, knocked off his plinth after he was hit by a van in 1971 and vandalised in 1979 and again in 1981 when he was doused in paint. In March 1986, Bobby was removed from his plinth again – but this time it was for repairs to be carried out at the workshop of Charles Henshaw and Sons. He remains one of the city's best-loved landmarks.

EMPIRE THEATRE

The longest continuous theatre site in the UK

Artists have been performing at the site of the old Empire Theatre since 1830, making this the longest continuous theatre site in the UK. The Nicolson Street theatre had several incarnations before the Empire Palace Theatre was opened by Edward Moss in November 1892. Designed by architect Frank Matcham, it accommodated an audience of up to 3,000 people on three lavishly decorated tiers. The theatre became a draw for some of the world's biggest stars including Charlie Chaplin and Anna Pavlova. Disaster struck in 1911 when a fire started on stage during a performance by the illusionist, The Great Lafayette. The theatre rose from the ashes, however, and even managed to survive competition from 'talking pictures'. This image was taken on 1 October 1928 to mark the reopening of the Empire Theatre with the musical *Showboat*. The Empire remained a popular theatre and music hall venue, with stars including Laurel and Hardy, Margo Fonteyn, and Judy Garland appearing.

The theatre became a major venue for the Edinburgh International Festival until 1963. From 1963 to 1991, however, the Empire was used as a bingo hall. In June 1994 the venue was once again transformed when the Festival Theatre opened. The theatre has a modern glass facade but retains the 1928 Empire Theatre's auditorium, and the dates 1928 and 1994 are carved above the proscenium arch. It is the largest performance area in Scotland and home to the national ballet and opera companies, Scottish Ballet and Scottish Opera, as well as being a major Edinburgh Festival venue.

THE THEATRE ROYAL AND
ST MARY'S CATHEDRAL

St Mary's is the principal place of worship for Roman Catholics in Edinburgh

Left: Edinburgh's original Theatre Royal was at Shakespeare Square, where it opened in 1769 at a cost of £5,000. It was demolished in 1860 to make way for the General Post Office at the corner of Waterloo Place and North Bridge. The theatre moved to a new home at the top of Broughton Street in 1876. This site had actually been home to a theatre since 1809, when it opened as Corri's Rooms, though it was renamed twice, as the Caledonian and the Adelphi. In 1853, it burnt down and was rebuilt as the Queen's Theatre and Opera House but in 1865 it was destroyed by fire again. By the time this photograph was taken in 1951, the theatre was lying derelict, and it was demolished in 1970. Just beyond the theatre building we can see St Mary's RC Cathedral. Designed by James Gillespie Graham in a Gothic Revival style, it opened as the Chapel of St Mary's in 1814 and became a cathedral in 1878. It was a replacement for a chapel at Blackfriar's Wynd which was burnt down by a mob, but it too was damaged by fire and had to be largely rebuilt in 1891.

Above: The demolition of the Theatre Royal has dramatically opened up our view of St Mary's RC Cathedral, which has been able to expand into part of the old theatre site. Its porch and baptistery were removed and a more spacious porch installed, and after a series of alterations, only the frontage remains of Gillespie Graham's original building. The cathedral, which is the principal place of worship for Roman Catholics in the city, was honoured to receive a visit from Pope John Paul II in 1982. The structure is dwarfed by the St James Centre, just visible to the left of this picture. Fortunately, plans for an urban motorway skirting the centre were abandoned. The Theatre Royal is still remembered by the pub of the same name, next to the nearby Playhouse Theatre at Greenside Place.

LEITH STREET

St James Square was almost entirely demolished to make way for the St James Centre

Left: This image, shot in the 1960s, shows the top of Leith Street, where it meets Princes Street (left) and Waterloo Place (right). Demolition work has already begun to clear the site for the building of the St James Centre. The development saw one of the earliest parts of the New Town, James Craig's St James Square, almost totally demolished, while Leith Street Terrace, which featured a split level row of houses and shops, loosely based on designs by Robert Adam, was completely razed. There was much opposition to the development at the time, particularly from the Cockburn Association, the city's civic trust, and the Royal Fine Art Commission for Scotland, who criticised its 'poor civic qualities, general lack of architectural merit, inappropriate bulk and volume, and impact on traffic flow'.

Above: Without Waterloo Place, this part of Edinburgh would be rather difficult to recognise from the 1960s photograph. From this vantage point, we can only see part of the St James Centre, which not only takes up most of the western side of Leith Street, but dominates views of the city centre from Leith Walk. The bridge, which is a recent replacement of the original, connects the shopping precinct with Calton Hill. The vista is closed by the Calton Square office development at Greenside Row. The building, designed in 1998, has filled a longstanding gapsite created when nineteenth-century tenements were demolished for a tunnel through Calton Hill that was never built.

St James Square was named after the architect James Craig, who drew up the first blueprint for the neoclassical-style New Town. The square was built during the 1770s as part of the first phase of construction. This photograph, from the archives of *The Scotsman* newspaper, was taken in 1956 when St James Square was still a base for several city-centre offices. It was almost completely demolished in 1965 to clear the way for the St James Centre and New St Andrew's House. While St James Square was not quite so elegant as its neighbouring Georgian thoroughfares, its architectural significance ensured that plans to knock it down to build a shopping and office complex were met with an angry outcry. One campaigner described the planned redevelopment as an 'Alcatraz'.

ST JAMES SQUARE

Named after James Craig who designed Edinburgh's New Town

While this picture is not taken from the same vantage point, most of St James Square has been obliterated by the sheer bulk of the St James Centre, here viewed from Leith Street. The building, which was officially opened by the Queen in 1975, has been repeatedly voted the worst in Edinburgh, with the Cockburn Association describing it as 'one of the monstrosities of modern Europe'. A repeat of such an unsympathetic development now seems unthinkable, following the designation of the Old and New Towns as a UNESCO World Heritage site. The St James Centre is now earmarked for demolition. Henderson Global Investors purchased the centre in 2006 and, at the time of writing, had submitted plans to the City of Edinburgh Council for an £850-million redevelopment of the site. Dubbed the 'St James Quarter', the proposals include a shopping centre, two hotels, 250 homes, offices, cafés and restaurants. If approved, work could start in 2011, with the development provisionally scheduled for completion in 2016.

BERNARD STREET, LEITH

The burgh of Leith was subsumed into Edinburgh in 1920

Left: Taken around the turn of the last century, this photograph shows Bernard Street, one of Leith's most elegant thoroughfares. A stone's throw from The Shore, this photograph has been taken at the street's wide junction with Constitution Street and Baltic Street. At the commercial and banking heart of Leith, Bernard Street was built in an area previously known as Bernard's Nook, which is thought to have been named after Bernard Lindsay of Lochill, a favourite of James VI. The statue silhouetted on the right is of the poet Robert Burns, who spent some time in Leith, and was sculpted by David Watson Stevenson in 1898. The cobbled street must have made for a bone-shaking experience on a bicycle, but the tram lines on the road are a sign that modern transport has arrived.

Above: Leith was subsumed into Edinburgh in 1920, 87 years after it had gained official independence and set up its own town council. Four out of five Leithers are said to have been against the merger. More than any other former town or village in the city, however, it retains its own identity and many people who live there consider themselves to be from Leith and not Edinburgh. During the most recent changes to constituency boundaries, the *Edinburgh Evening News* successfully campaigned for Leith's name to be retained on the electoral map. Bernard Street was restored in the 1980s, with many of its former banks renovated, and the centre of old Leith has been given a facelift. In recent years, stylish bars have opened on the street, and many locals see no need to journey into the centre of Edinburgh for a night out.

GREAT JUNCTION STREET, LEITH

Built to speed up the transportation of goods between Leith and Edinburgh

Left: Great Junction Street runs from the foot of Leith Walk towards the Water of Leith and Leith Docks. It was built in the early nineteenth century to speed up the transportation of goods between Leith and Edinburgh. Tenements line both sides of the street, with rows of shops at street level. By the 1870s, Great Junction Street was a main route for horse-drawn trams which connected Haymarket and Princes Street to Leith. One of the first horse-drawn trams was operated by John Brown, of Iona Street, whose route connected Newhaven and Morningside. In 1905, Leith made the switch from horse-drawn trams to electric trams – seen in the centre of this photograph, taken around the time of their introduction. Unfortunately Edinburgh was only using cable car trams at the time, so passengers who wanted to travel out of Leith needed to change between the two services.

Above: While not in the heart of the old port, Great Junction Street's transport links to the rest of the city have made this the main shopping area in Leith. However, the area still suffers significant levels of poverty and deprivation. In recent decades, Great Junction Street has suffered a decline and the thoroughfare has yet to show much visible benefit from Leith's recent regeneration. At the time of writing, there was disruption to traffic in the area during work to reinstate trams to Leith Walk. The first phase of the route, due to start operation in 2011, will connect Edinburgh Airport to Newhaven.

THE SHORE, LEITH

Built around a natural harbour at the mouth of the Water of Leith

Left: Taken in the 1860s, this is one of the earliest photographic images of The Shore. Built around a natural harbour at the mouth of the Water of Leith, The Shore used to be on the sea, but was effectively moved further inland following the development of Leith docks, starting in the late eighteenth century. Historically Leith was Scotland's main port, and was the landing point for visiting royalty arriving by sea. It was even a brief home to the royal court during the regency of Mary of Guise, mother of Mary, Queen of Scots, in the sixteenth century. In this photograph, we can see a more mundane aspect of everyday life in Victorian Leith, with a fishmarket in full swing in the foreground. The bridge to the left of the picture connects Commercial Street and Bernard Street.

Above: While The Shore is still recognisable from the days of the Victorians, the area had fallen into a steep decline, particularly after the post-war demise of the shipbuilding industry, and gained a reputation for seediness and slum conditions. Since the 1980s, however, the area has undergone significant regeneration. Derelict tenements have been restored and warehouses converted into modern high-end apartments. The area around The Shore is now a fashionable address – unthinkable a generation ago. Leith's resurgence has been boosted by significant developments, led by Forth Ports building of a new headquarters for the Scottish Government at nearby Victoria Quay, the construction of the Ocean Terminal shopping mall designed by Sir Terence Conran, and the decision to dock the former Royal Yacht *Britannia* in Leith. The Queen's old yacht is now a major tourist attraction.

INNER HARBOUR, LEITH

Leith was still a thriving independent burgh when this 1902 photo was taken

Left: This photograph of The Shore was taken around 1902, looking back towards Edinburgh, when the port of Leith was still thriving as an independent burgh. Leith's maritime history is symbolised by the imposing harbour signal tower, on the far left of the picture. This was built in 1686 by the King's master mason, Robert Mylne. It was originally a windmill, and later became the signal tower. The building was converted in the early 1800s when the original roof was removed and the windows and battlements added to fortify it during the Napoleonic Wars. Leith's fishing tradition depended on a plentiful supply of white fish, lobster and oysters. As well as fishing and trading ships, Leith was also a centre for whaling, with ships travelling thousands of miles in search of their lucrative catch. Leith Harbour, on the island of South Georgia, is named after the Scottish port.

Above: No fishing boats are now based in Leith, though Robert Mylne's harbour signal tower is now the oldest surviving building on The Shore. Many of the tenements from the archive picture have survived, despite falling into slum conditions during much of the twentieth century. A stone's throw from Mylne's signal tower is the chic Malmaison Hotel, a conversion of an old sailors' mission, originally built in 1833. There is a harpoon memorial to Leith's whaling history near the hotel. The Shore area now boasts a number of top restaurants, many of which fittingly specialise in fish and seafood dishes.

THE KING'S WARK, LEITH

The original King's Wark was built for James I and formed part of Leith's defences

Left: This view of The Shore taken in the 1950s shows the King's Wark, the light-coloured building on the corner of Bernard Street. The original King's Wark was built for James I in the fifteenth century, and formed part of Leith's defences. The tower house was an arsenal and grain store, and also served as a hospital during the plague outbreak in the late sixteenth century. It was redeveloped for James VI to include a tennis court. This building was destroyed by fire in the late seventeenth century and this picture shows the eighteenth-century tenement built on the same site. The building in baronial style on the far left of the picture was built in 1865 by J. Anderson Hamilton.

Above: While The Shore is still recognisable today there have been some significant changes. The eighteenth-century King's Wark building has survived, but only the ground floor of the tenement building next door at No. 37 remains. The rest of the building was demolished in the early 1970s and rebuilt. The old ironmongers and chandlers that thrived during Leith's heyday as a port and centre for shipbuilding are now more likely to be restaurants and bars. The ground floor of No. 37 recently became home to a branch of Pizza Express, and some of the city's finest restaurants, including Restaurant Martin Wishart which is at No. 54, are in this area. The history of the site is remembered by the name of the bar, The King's Wark, on the ground floor at the corner of Bernard Street.

DONALDSON'S COLLEGE

William Henry Playfair's Elizabethan-style building opened in 1851

Left: One of the most striking buildings in the entire city is Donaldson's College at West Coates, near Haymarket. This vast Gothic structure opened in 1851 as a 'hospital' school for orphans. It was built with a bequest from the printer and bookseller James Donaldson, whose name is still carved above the entrance. The competition to find an architect called for an Elizabethan design, and William Henry Playfair duly took his inspiration from Elizabethan manor houses, such as Burleigh House in Northamptonshire. His design is also thought to have been influenced by that of the seventeenth-century George Heriot's School in the Lauriston area of Edinburgh. In 1938, Donaldson's school merged with the Royal Edinburgh Institution for the Deaf and Dumb, and its intake was restricted to deaf pupils.

Above: Donaldson's College has become a world leader in the education of deaf children. In 2003, however, the school was deemed too old-fashioned for modern educational needs, and too expensive to maintain. The school's trust decided to move to new premises at Linlithgow in West Lothian, and the building was sold to developers Cala Homes. Richard Murphy Architects came up with a blueprint for converting the grade-A listed structure while retaining its character. RMA produced a design to transform the 'Gothic fantasy' interior into around 70 flats. It has been proposed that the redevelopment of Donaldson's will also involve building another 70 flats to the north of the school. RMA's intention was to leave the impressive views of Donaldson's College unspoilt for future generations to enjoy.

CRAIGLOCKHART HYDROPATHIC HOSPITAL / NAPIER UNIVERSITY

Poets Siegfried Sassoon and Wilfred Owen met at Craiglockhart in 1917

Left: Craiglockhart Hydropathic Hospital opened as a sanatorium in 1880. Described as a 'giant Italian villa', the building was designed by architects Peddie & Kinnear, complete with a 15m by 7m swimming pool and Turkish baths. In addition to water treatments at the hospital, guests were also able to take part in activities such as archery, bowling, croquet, golf or lawn-tennis, or simply stroll in its 12-acre gardens on Wester Craiglockhart Hill in the south west of Edinburgh. The hospital was requisitioned during World War I, and between 1916 and 1919 it was used to treat officers for shell shock. It was here that Dr W.H.R. Rivers and Dr Arthur Brock pioneered the treatment of post-traumatic stress disorder. They are pictured in the inset – Rivers is sixth from the left and Brock sixth from the right in the front row. Poets Siegfried Sassoon and Wilfred Owen met at Craiglockhart in 1917, and Sassoon is widely thought to have had a positive influence on the younger man's work.

Above: Napier College – now Napier University – acquired the building in 1984 and opened its Craiglockhart campus three years later. While the interior has been significantly altered to accommodate the needs of teaching staff and students, the exterior is well-preserved, and the building retains spacious gardens. As well as the university's business school, Craiglockhart houses the War Poets Collection, and commemorates its pivotal role in producing some of Britain's best known war poets with a permanent exhibition. During the 1990s, the story of Rivers, Owen and Sassoon inspired Pat Barker's award-winning *Regeneration* trilogy – comprising the novels *Regeneration*, *The Eye in the Door* and *The Ghost Road* – with many scenes set at Craiglockhart and other parts of Edinburgh. In 1997, *Regeneration* was made into a film starring Jonathan Pryce and Jonny Lee Miller.

THE FORTH BRIDGE

Fowler and Baker's steel bridge was a marvel of engineering when it opened in 1890

Left: One of the most iconic structures in the world, the Forth Bridge was a marvel of engineering at the time of its construction. As the world's first major steel bridge, its distinctive cantilever structure was designed to distribute load more evenly and safely. Certainly the engineers, Sir John Fowler and Sir Benjamin Baker, would have been anxious to avoid any repeat of the Tay Bridge disaster. The Tay Bridge collapsed on 28 December 1879 killing 75 train passengers. Literally thousands of men were involved in building the bridge, which connects South Queensferry near Edinburgh with North Queensferry in Fife – one of Scotland's busiest crossing points for 1,000 years. The bridge was opened by Edward, Prince of Wales in 1890, and its importance as a major transport link was later underlined by the fact that the Germans attempted to bomb it during World War II. The passenger ferries shown in this 1955 photograph were no longer required after the nearby Forth Road Bridge opened in 1964.

Above: For more than a century, the Forth Bridge has been carrying countless passenger and freight trains safely across the Firth of Forth estuary. The bridge has also become a major tourist attraction with coach loads of visitors regularly stopping off in South Queensferry to enjoy spectacular views of the bridge. In recent years, there have been fresh efforts to find out more about the men who lost their lives building it. Around 70 men lost their lives during the construction work and a memorial to their sacrifice was unveiled by First Minister Alex Salmond in South Queensferry in 2007. At the time, Mr Salmond described the bridge as a 'blood red wonder'. Due to the high volume of commuter and commercial traffic now using the road and rail bridges, a second Forth Road Bridge is being proposed by the Scottish Government.